A SHORT COURSE IN ADVERTISING

BY
ALEX F. OSBORN, Ph.M.
VICE-PRESIDENT BARTON, DURSTINE & OSBORN, INC.
FORMERLY INSTRUCTOR IN SALES AND ADVERTISING IN HUTCHINSON HIGH SCHOOL
AND ASSOCIATION INSTITUTE, BUFFALO, N. Y.

WITH PREFACE BY
MAC MARTIN
CHAIRMAN, AGENCY SERVICE COMMITTEE OF THE AMERICAN ASSOCIATION OF
ADVERTISING AGENCIES
PROFESSORIAL LECTURER IN ADVERTISING, UNIVERSITY OF MINNESOTA
FORMERLY CHAIRMAN OF RESEARCH COMMITTEE OF THE ASSOCIATED ADVERTISING CLUBS
OF THE WORLD
EX-PRESIDENT OF MINNEAPOLIS ADVERTISING FORUM

WITH ILLUSTRATIONS

1921

TO
MY WIFE

AUTHOR'S NOTE

This book reflects a study of the work of a thousand or more men, crystallized in my own experience in the advertising of some thirty different products, involving an annual expenditure of over a million.

The mother of this book is necessity—the necessity I felt for some simple, comprehensive text while I served as a teacher. This strongly inclined me to attempt the preparation of such a text. Later this inclination was aggravated by contact with men who spend millions on advertising: I made the attempt and now offer the result in the hope that those captains of business, as well as the novices, may care to view the inner "works" of advertising.

Certain men have definitely helped. Each chapter has been revised and corrected, by an expert who seemed best fitted in each phase.

CONTENTS

INTRODUCTION BY MAC MARTIN

CHAPTER		PAGE
I.	HOW ADVERTISING AIDS CIVILIZATION	1
II.	NAME-PUBLICITY VERSUS PERSUASIVE-ADVERTISING	8
III.	THE TRADE-MARK AS A MENTAL PEG	12
IV.	ANALYZING THE PROBLEM	19
V.	WHAT WORDS WORK BEST ON THE PROSPECT	30
VI.	SUGGESTION—THE MOTIVE POWER OF ADVERTISING	39
VII.	WAYS TO WIN ATTENTION	47
VIII.	HOW DO SIZE AND COLOR AID DISPLAY?	55
IX.	PRINTING PROCESSES, PLATES, AND PAPERS	64
X.	TYPE AND TYPOGRAPHICAL ARRANGEMENT	76
XI.	VISUALIZING THE ADVERTISING MESSAGE	86
XII.	PRELIMINARY ANALYSIS BY THE RETAIL ADVERTISER	95
XIII.	ANALYSIS OF RETAIL APPEAL	102
XIV.	METHODS OF RETAIL ADVERTISING	109
XV.	ADVERTISING'S PART IN DEPARTMENT STORES	117
XVI.	WHO AND WHERE ARE THE BEST PROSPECTS?	125
XVII.	ANALYSIS OF THE CONSUMER'S ATTITUDE	132

CONTENTS

CHAPTER		PAGE
XVIII.	Methods of Distribution	138
XIX.	Retail Branches and Exclusive Agencies	145
XX.	Producer — Jobber — Dealer Distribution	150
XXI.	Consumer Advertising Which Enlists the Dealer	156
XXII.	Advertising—Plus Sales Work	162
XXIII.	The Salesman and the Advertising	169
XXIV.	Planning a General Campaign	174
XXV.	Continuity Through a Central Thought	181
XXVI.	Factors in the Selection of Media	187
XXVII.	The Daily Newspaper as a Medium	194
XXVIII.	Sunday Newspapers and Newspaper Co-operation	200
XXIX.	Magazines, Class and Trade Publications	204
XXX.	Street-Car, Theatre, and Outdoor Media	209
XXXI.	Demonstrating, Sampling, and Sales Aids	216
XXXII.	The Dealer's Store as a Medium	222
XXXIII.	The Mail as a Medium	227
XXXIV.	A Typical National Campaign	232
XXXV.	A Typical Localized Campaign	239
	Index	245

INTRODUCTION

Benjamin Franklin was a man with great vision. I wonder, on that memorable night when he and his son were flying their little silk kite out in the storm, whether he could see the thing which he was collecting in his Leyden jar as we use it to-day.

It is less than one hundred and seventy years since Franklin's experiments, yet to-day we use this power to assist in almost every field of human endeavor. It heats our houses. It drives our locomotives. It lights our cities. It makes the deaf hear and the blind see. It even resuscitates the drowning. As soon as this power was captured, controlled, and directed, it became so much a part of the daily life of man that now we can hardly imagine a world without it.

Advertising, like electricity, is indefinable. It is a power which moves minds as electricity moves elements. It runs in a current; it has momentum; it is founded on the magnetism of character just as electricity is founded on the magnetism of matter.

The other day I saw a great crane lift some enormous steel girders to the top of a tall building. Nothing held them to the crane but this fluid power we call electricity. In a moment some one pressed a button somewhere and the girders fell. The power had been released. The big steel surface of the crane was, in itself, helpless to retain them.

The other day I was looking through the pages of an old magazine and I came across an advertisement long forgotten. I recalled the day when the name of the thing there advertised was a household word throughout the length and breadth of the land. A few years ago some one had pressed a button somewhere. The true power of advertising had been shut off. The maker tried everything he could to lift the name again, but his advertising was gone as completely and permanently as the power of the magnetic crane.

INTRODUCTION

Concentrating a message into an advertisement is much like charging a Leyden jar. A man never fully realizes what his undertaking is until he begins to put his mind on paper. When one begins to picture a thing as he wishes the world to see it, he has taken the first step toward making the thing as he would have the world know it.

Advertising is that electrifying power which takes these vague notions we have and changes them into policies we are willing to fight for.

Advertising is the power which electrifies the salesman, the wholesaler, and the dealer into a spirit of service beyond the mere sale.

Just as in electricity Franklin proved the power of points to conduct, Volta demonstrated the ability of the current to travel, Faraday discovered the power of currents to rotate, and Edison turned the spark into a steady light—so to-day energetic advertising men are giving their lives in an effort to add little by little and step by step to the world's knowledge of this great omnipresent power which we call advertising.

The book which you are about to read analyzes and explains the secrets of this great force. It is not filled with theories of what might be done. It shows what is being done. It takes up the things we now know one by one and explains the whys so that the same things may be done again. It tells how this power may be captured, controlled, and directed. Read it carefully not only for the words but for the thoughts it makes you see between the lines. It is for you to direct the power you thus master. It is for you to find new uses perhaps heretofore undreamed.

Mr. Osborn, the author, has been one of the most active participants in this new development. His advertising has helped to turn an unknown brand into a world-leader. In several instances he has helped to nationalize local industries and make possible in five years the progress that would have required twenty years without the electrification of advertising.

As an instructor in Sales and Advertising in Hutchinson

High School and the Association Institute of Buffalo, he has given his time and his ideas freely that others might profit by his work. A close student of business conditions, he has developed some of the most successful advertising plans of the last decade. He is Vice-President of Barton, Durstine & Osborn, an advertising agency which handles some thirty of the notable advertising campaigns of to-day.

If you obtain from this book the pleasure and profit which I have, I think you will agree with me that the world is starting to control, direct, and use the force of advertising fully as effectively as it has used that other great indefinable force, electricity.

MAC MARTIN.

February 28, 1921.

A SHORT COURSE IN
ADVERTISING

CHAPTER I

How Advertising Aids Civilization

Why does advertising hold the centre of the business stage to-day? Why is it so fascinating? Is it because of its magnitude—the fact that it represents a yearly expenditure of a billion or more? No. Its appeal is greater than that of mere volume. Its lure lies in its unfathomable mystery, in its Aladdin-like power. For advertising never can be cut-and-dried. So long as human nature remains infinitely variable, there can be no rule-of-thumb methods of advertising; for human nature is the raw material upon which it must work. Advertising is therefore not a *science* but an art, based upon a set of principles originating in theories, and crystallized by experience.

To define it more specifically would be difficult, but is it not also unnecessary for our purpose? We do not care whether it can best be termed "the art of creating a new want," as one authority would have it, or whether its true definition is both more specific and more extensive than that. For instance, a thing that is keenly wanted, such as bread, can nevertheless be advertised, yet, there is no "creation of a new want" for such a commodity. To define advertising, therefore, you must employ some more inclusive phrase. But broadly and practically speaking, it is printed salesmanship —and salesmanship is the business of disposing of goods at a profit.

Advertising is costly. Its only justification is that it makes money. For most advertisers it is profitable, for others it is ruinous. The aim is to find why one method will win, while another will lose. Always, the test is the profit—that is resulting sales that yield an increased net margin in favor of the advertiser—whether that profit be judged by immediate

A SHORT COURSE IN ADVERTISING

results or by the gradual results that come with the building of good will. Profit, direct or indirect, that is the alpha and omega of advertising.

Although advertising is designed solely to bring greater profit to the advertiser, it may likewise result in increased value to the consumer; and this result justifies advertising from the standpoint of economic desirability. But that point is difficult to grasp. I remember that when a boy of seventeen, I had to write an oration on "Economic Waste in America," and I then thought that advertising belonged in that rogue's gallery. Since then I have seen it result to the consumer's advantage with more than 100 different kinds of products in the exploitation of which I have worked.

Advertising is the child of modern conditions. Modern competition is the cause of its present great volume. Formerly, favorable word-of-mouth comment and discussion gave the local merchant all the business he could handle "without hiring extra clerks." Then the mail-order business developed, and the giant "catalogue" houses began to undersell the local dealer. He found it hard to "compete," simply because he had never known aggressive competition. He had not been doing enough business in proportion to his rent and other fixed expenses—charges that taxed his business to about the same degree, whether he sold $100 or $1,000 worth a month.

So the local merchant began to advertise. And his competitor advertised. Competition made them both buy more closely. Competition made them both fight for more business. And, getting more business, they were better able to compete —not only with each other, but with those outside businesses which so aggressively sought to take the trade away from home. The upshot was such that the alert local merchant can now compete, because, through advertising, he can now sell so much more merchandise, that his cost of doing business has gone down from 50%, or thereabouts, to where today it averages, the country over, less than 30%, inclusive of a considerable advertising "expense."

Shining examples may be given which shed a clear light

on this truth: A shoe store, spending $10,000 a year on advertising, has been able to double its business. Buying twice as many shoes, it can now buy closer. But that is not all. On its former volume of $100,000 the fixed expenses were about $30,000 or 30%. On double the volume, its fixed expenses are the same, plus $10,000 for advertising, or about $40,000 all told. Thus the cost of doing business is now 20% instead of 30%. And the merchant can now sell a pair of shoes, which cost him $4.00, at a retail price of $5.50, and make more money than he formerly could by selling the same pair at $6.20. This means a 70 cents saving for the consumer, and 6 cents greater profit to the seller!

Likewise, most manufacturers are grasping the golden opportunity that judicious advertising offers. For instance, a plant that has been doing a business of $350,000 per year used to have twenty drummers running about the country to sell that output. These twenty salesmen cost approximately $50,000 per year, and they merely scratched the surface of the potential market. At last the manufacturer decided to take a chance. He let ten of the salesmen go and appropriated $15,000 for advertising. Now his volume of business is even bigger. Instead of $50,000 his selling now costs him only $40,000, and accordingly the public benefits.

But the greatest saving to the consumer comes when the manufacturer becomes a benevolent giant. In advertising one such business—the biggest of its kind in the world—$300,000 a year is spent. The product is one that everybody needs. Many a woman who sees the large advertisements, says: "My—if they would only cut the price of their goods, instead of wasting so much money on advertising."

That is the fallacy. This is the fact: In each $1.00 worth of goods about one cent goes to advertising. This mounts up to $300,000 on a $30,000,000 business. An increase of $10,000,000 in one year has resulted. The manufacturer has been able to put 10% more into raw materials and to pay 25% higher wages. In other words, a 1% expenditure on advertising has resulted in more than 25% greater income to the employees and considerably more than 10% better value to the consumer. And, in addition, the manufacturer made a profit which, without that expenditure on advertising, would have been well-nigh impossible.

When a large cereal manufacturer came out with an announcement that in the future every package was to be covered with a wax cover some would-be economists said: "Phew—how can they so increase the cost of their goods and not raise the price?" The answer is simple. So big has their volume of business become as a result of advertising (according to their own statement) that they are able not only to lower the price but also to give a larger package, and on top of that, a better box. That is how advertising increases the purchasing power of the average consumer's dollar.

Additional public benefits come from two other sources:

First, the retail merchant who handles this manufacturer's output is willing to sell it at a smaller margin than he would require of an unadvertised article. He is willing to "sacrifice" part of his gross profit in this way, because he needs to expend less effort in selling the kind for which a demand has been created through advertising.

Second, advertising benefits the public because the manufacturer who advertises has to be more careful. He has to be surer that his goods are up to a high standard. He knows that advertised products are subject to much more severe scrutiny from the ultimate purchaser than are those for which no claims are published.

Decreased selling expense enables a manufacturer to lower his price, cost of labor and materials permitting; and, as a rule, he wants to lower his price so as to lift his volume of business to the highest possible point and thus secure the maximum net revenue from the sale of his output.

Some advertising does create new wants; and new wants make possible new elements of civilization. Have you ever realized that the laborer of to-day enjoys more luxuries than the mightiest king of the middle ages? Ten cents takes you to the movies. You drink in with your own eyes the beauties of the Alps—a gay scene in Hawaii—a laughing comedy of the world's funniest clowns—all in a short evening. Any

A Fairy Soap advertisement of twenty years ago (lower right) and one of now.
Think how this constant education toward cleanliness has glorified bathing, and has thus aided health and morals and the other ingredients of civilization.

ancient king would have offered part of his empire to sit for one evening in that seat of yours. And the 5-cent weekly magazine which you read—so much as a matter of course—Julius Cæsar would have offered a part of Gaul for as much instruction and entertainment as you can absorb, sitting in your favorite arm-chair, on a Friday evening.

Without advertising, that magazine would probably cost you its weight in gold. Fifty thousand dollars could not buy the mere manuscripts and art-work in a single issue. Without advertising, moving-pictures could not have taken their present place in human life. Advertising insured to moving-picture enterprises a quick volume of business—great enough to distribute the giant first-costs over the masses of population, thereby making the movies financially available to the millions.

Entertainment and culture have come to the ears of all on the wings of music. How much would a Victrola cost to-day if advertising had not made possible the present huge production, running into hundreds of thousands of talking-machines per year? Instead of almost every family having Caruso, Mary Garden, Kreisler, Paderewski, and all the world's foremost artists in their own homes, only the millionaire could afford a talking-machine if advertising had not created a well-nigh universal market for mechanical music.

Morals bear a direct relation to mind, and mind is the mirror of health. Suppose that none of us cleaned our teeth for three years—what would be the state of our health? Suppose no one bathed for three years—would not our bodies and minds degenerate? And if health failed, and cleanliness ceased, to what level would our morals decline?

The advertising of dentifrice and tooth-brushes has taught our nation the value and pleasure of tooth hygiene. The advertising of soap and plumbing has made us take more kindly to bathing. When twenty million men shave themselves each morning to come to breakfast brighter, cleaner, and more smiling, is it an exaggeration to say that in this respect alone advertising has justified itself sociologically?

The correspondence courses, advanced executive training like that of the Alexander Hamilton Institute, the spread of good literature, like Doctor Eliot's five-foot book-shelf—all these and thousands of other boons are distinct steps forward in our civilization, and all are made possible by advertising.

And in the material needs of man, advertising has given us more and better clothes, and homes, and food, because advertising has helped increase the human capacity for production. Think how your own daily life has been enhanced by the tractor, the truck, the plough, the typewriter, the adding-machine, the electric light, the stationary engine—the many thousands of labor-saving inventions which advertising has quickly brought into economical and general use.

In the crises of civilization advertising now stands shoulder-to-shoulder with armies and navies. Could the spirit that won the Great War have been inspired without advertising? The Red Cross could not have financed its work, the Liberty Loans could not have been raised, food-saving could not have been inculcated in the people if advertising had not won the minds of the millions.

Like all high-powered agencies, advertising may be dangerous in the hands of the bad. Just as dynamite may be used to turn worthless swamps into fields of golden wheat, or may be misused to blow up a children's hospital, so is it with advertising. But advertising cannot long be misused to propagate evil doctrines, for advertising is its own safety-valve.

This is because, just as no worthless product can stand advertising for any length of time, so no falsehood can be permanently spread by advertising. Publicity sheds a white light on that which it promotes, a light so searching as to show up, sooner or later, the least rottenness that exists, whether it be in a product or propaganda.

CHAPTER II

Name-Publicity versus Persuasive-Advertising

Advertising may be roughly divided into two kinds:
1. Name-Advertising.
2. Persuasive-Advertising.

The nature of the product will determine which is the better to use. Name-Advertising simply aims at the familiarization and popularization of a name, a slogan, a trade-mark, or a package. By employing it the advertiser hopes through emphasis to stamp his product on the subconscious mind of the consumer. Name-Advertising does not seek any direct action. It is content to familiarize—to build up prestige—gradually, insidiously, and cumulatively.

Persuasive-Advertising is quite different in its aim and method. While it seeks to establish a familiarity with, and a favorable attitude toward, the product advertised—incidentally to impress its brand and familiarize its name—its great purpose is to persuade and to convince.

Persuasive-Advertising seeks either to get the consumer to send for more information, as a step toward an ultimate purchase, or to get the consumer to go and buy the product without further ado—or at least to feel a real desire for that particular product in preference to all others in the field of competition.

Name-Advertising is the kind of advertising which you usually see on the bill-boards, on the electric signs, in the street-cars, and in other places where the message must be read at a glance. Always, it is only suggestive: the name of the article is the emphatic key-note of the message. Beyond that it merely hints at some reason why you should buy.

There are as many words in the twenty-year-old Armour advertisement at lower right, as in the new one at top. But the latter is "Persuasive Advertising"—and the old-timer is "Name-Publicity." The illustrations in the new advertisement furnish the persuasion.

Persuasive-Advertising, on the other hand, has to do much more than that. It cannot accomplish its purpose by merely attracting the eye. It has four functions:

1. To attract the eye.
2. To arouse the interest.
3. To move the judgment.
4. To open the purse.

Argument, plus persuasive suggestion—in other words, "reason-why" copy—that is what Persuasive-Advertising is made of. It must be where it can be read. Its message must impel to action. It must carry a stronger, more immediate appeal, than any mere name-emphasis does. It cannot be read on the run.

An analysis of your product and prospect should determine whether you should use Persuasive-Advertising (with "reason-why" "copy") or Name-Advertising (with merely suggestive copy). Sometimes an article may need the former at first, and later can be successfully promoted through non-persuasive—simply suggestive—Name-Advertising. But even then, other things being equal, Persuasive-Advertising is preferable, for by this method to-morrow's sales may pay for to-day's advertising, and good-will, instead of being the mere knowledge of a name, may become a public conviction and faith concerning the distinctive qualities of the product which the name represents.

The general tendency is toward Persuasive-Advertising, because usually this method impresses the trade-name quite as well as Name-Advertising, and in addition, by way of excess value, plants in the public mind a definite feeling of positive favor toward the product advertised.

"Quaker Oats" used to be "pushed" through Name-Publicity. Emphasis of the trade-name was the backbone of the advertising. Why not? It sounded reasonable. Every family used oats. All that seemed necessary was to shout the name "Quaker" loud enough and often enough. But the plan shifted, and to-day Quaker products occupy more than a million dollars' worth of space each year in magazine advertisements which explain in pictures and words just why and how Quaker products are cheaper and better than other competitive foodstuffs. That is but one of many instances where Persuasive-Advertising has been finally preferred. Under the old method the name occupied 90% of the space. Under the new, the name takes only a small fraction; but still it is so prominent that if you but glance at a Quaker Oats "ad" you will see the trade-name. Above all, you will receive that suggestion, that "reason-why" which *persuades* as well as reminds.

In fact, competition has necessitated more and better Persuasive-Advertising. In the old days, if you painted the name of your soap on elephants' backs, on barn roofs, on flat rocks and wooden fences, you were a great advertiser. But what chance would soap so advertised have now against Lux, and Woodbury's, and Ivory, and the other brands which make such intriguing and persuasive "reason-why" appeals? Many products are known by name, many products are on the lips of the millions—so many, that if yours is not in the heart, as well as on the lips of the consumer, it will not be bought.

Emphasize the name certainly; but don't forget that you might shout "Jones' Hams" for ever and ever into the ears of your prospects, and yet they would think no more favorably of them. Make the name known, but remember that in order to sell you must first persuade.

CHAPTER III

The Trade-Mark as a Mental Peg

Particularly in Name-Advertising, the keystone of any campaign is the trade-mark. This may be a coined name like "Uneeda," or it may be an actual name like "Ford," presented in connection with a distinctive design.

Especially in the national advertising of a manufacturer, a trade-mark is indispensable because the value of such advertising is not the mere sum of the separate values of each "ad." A greater value accumulates and piles up with continuity. This is called "cumulative" value. It increases geometrically with repetition. The arguments upon arguments—direct and indirect—which the advertiser builds up in favor of his goods, will fall short of their full efficiency unless they are associated with the trade-name or trade-mark of a particular brand of goods. The trade-name and trade-mark form a mental peg on which to hang the garments of superiority which advertising weaves in favor of the particular article.

What good would it do the manufacturers of Lux simply to advertise the virtues of soap flakes? They have made "Lux" mean soap flakes. In the case of Ivory Soap Flakes, the trade-mark is a combination of an old trade-name with the actual name of the kind of goods. In the case of a cleaning powder it is "Old Dutch Cleanser" (if the advertiser be Cudahy & Company), or it is "Gold Dust" (if the advertiser be N. K. Fairbanks).

Coined trade-names are sometimes so effectively impressed that they become parts of our vocabulary. Who would think Kodak was a coined name owned by the Eastman Company? And yet it is true—this statement of its significance is given by the Eastman Kodak Company: "In 1888 when two 'k's,' an 'o,' a 'd,' and an 'a' were first euphoniously assembled they meant nothing. Arranged to spell 'Kodak,' they now signify certain products of the Eastman Kodak Company, such as Kodak Cameras, Kodak Tripods, and Kodak Film Tanks. Kodak is our registered and common-law trade-mark and cannot be rightfully applied except to goods of our manufacture."

When trade-marks such as "Kodak" do become bywords they are worth fabulous sums. It is said that if Coca Cola were to be offered for sale to-day, that name of eight letters would bring over $4,000,000—over half a million dollars per letter. The name "Wrigley" in connection with chewing-gum is worth almost as many millions as it has letters. Think what a byword "Postum" has been made through Persuasive-Advertising, and you will see why any one who enters national advertising without a trade-mark which is distinctive, descriptive, easy to say, easy to remember, and of pleasant suggestion is very apt to fall short of maximum efficiency.

"But," as trade-mark attorney D. A. Woodcock has said, "no matter how attractive a mark or name may be, it is folly to spend money in advertising it unless the advertiser is to reap the benefit. If other persons are free to adopt the mark, his trade will be stolen and his advertisement will be worse than useless. His only safeguard is to select a valid trade-mark at the outset." Mr. Woodcock's definition of a trade-mark is: "Any symbol applied to goods which identifies in the public mind the manufacturer, merchant, or jobber, who makes or selects the goods and sells them." Advertising alone will not create trade-marks. They must be used on the goods sold. The valuable feature of the trade-mark is the reputation which it acquires through the belief of the public that that trade-mark points to the goods upon which it is used as being the product of some particular manufacturer, merchant, or jobber. The part of advertising is to link together in the mind of the public the trade-mark, its owner, the goods, and the superior qualities of the goods.

The other aspect of a trade-mark which the law considers is its quality of protecting the public against deception. For this last reason a trade-mark will not receive registration which resembles a trade-mark already adopted, or which describes the goods or their qualities. Such words as these have been rejected because considered descriptive: "COMPUTING" for Scales, "ELASTIC SEAM" for Drawers, and "FAULTLESS" for Bread as that is supposed to describe bread. On the other hand, the word Bond in Bond Bread is in the dictionary; but by selecting a name which though descriptive is not descriptive of bread, by being the first to use the name Bond as a mark for bread, by putting that word into a distinctive Old English lettering, by associating it with a bond guaranteeing the purity of a loaf of bread, the originators of that bread are protected; they have not only the common-law rights of priority, but also specific registration by the government patent office to prevent infringers from imitating.

Other marks which will not usually be protected or registered are those which consist merely of the name of an individual, firm, corporation or association not written in a distinctive manner, or which consist merely in a geographical name or term, like "New York Chocolates," or "New England Mackerel." These marks would ordinarily be the common property of all persons bearing similar names, or doing business in the same region.

Other trade-marks which cannot be legally adopted and protected are those which consist of or comprise flags or other insignia of the United States or other countries, fraternal emblems, or portraits of living individuals, without the consent of the person shown. Many other marks are proper subjects for appropriation, but are so commonplace in their nature as to have two disadvantages: one, that the public will not easily remember the mark as indicating a particular person or corporation; the other, that it may subsequently be discovered that other persons have previously adopted the mark and would be able to stop its use.

Of course, many trade-marks or names violate these rules and yet are protected despite that fact. But the establishment of their validity required years of use, good luck, and frequently long and expensive lawsuits. The business man who has not yet chosen his trade-mark should not gamble

THE TRADE-MARK AS A MENTAL PEG 15

upon the chance of equal luck; but should select a good legal trade-mark in the first place.

To insure maximum permanent protection a trade-mark should indicate its origin rather than the product itself. For instance, a word which has become the name for a certain kind of a patented product may not belong to the manufacturer in perpetuity. When the patents ran out on Aspirin, this name became available for use by any one who cared to manufacture according to the particular formula which was known to result in Aspirin. The original manufacturer had to change his trade-name from "Aspirin" to "Bayer's Aspirin" in order to indicate the product's origin.

Although "Pierce Arrow" is one of the best trade-names in existence (because it combines the idea of speed derived from the word "arrow" with the name of the manufacturer), the courts would probably not uphold the Pierce Company's rights on the name if another manufacturer named Pierce wished to make and sell "Pierce" cars.

The ideal trade-mark is one which consists in an unusual design or emblem, or in a novel or fanciful word, such as "KEDS" or "UNEEDA." If such a mark is selected, its novelty will be the best guarantee that no earlier user has acquired it, and the same novelty will lend itself well to advertising.

After a trade-mark has been selected, the next step is the application of that mark to the goods or containers, and their sale. This must precede any application for registration of the trade-mark, and should precede any advertising of the mark lest some outsider gain possession of the mark by actually using it on a product before the advertiser has done so. It is wise to register trade-marks in the U. S. Patent Office, for this simplifies the task of preventing infringement; but registration only establishes a presumption of the ownership, which is overthrown if another can prove that he was the first to use it. Even unregistered marks are protected in this country to some extent. In many foreign countries, however, any person who registers the trade-mark, rightly or wrongly, controls it.

Advertising prints and labels differ from trade-marks in that they are supposed to possess some slight artistic qualities, and are usually descriptive of the articles upon which the labels are to be placed, or in the advertisement of which prints are to be used. These should never be published or used without bearing the word "copyright" or the symbol ©, together with the name of the proprietor. After the print or label has been published or used bearing such a copyright notice, an application may be made for its registration.

Sometimes a trade-name may brand a whole family of products, like Colgate's toilet goods, or Heinz's canned goods, preserves, and pickles. There is danger in having too many trade-names or trade-marks. It is better to use a general trade-name as the common mark of many products. The manufacturer who tries to build good-will for several names weakens his advertising. Especially is it wasteful to advertise more than one brand at a time, for then each trade-mark so competes against the other that each has less than a proportionate chance to make its impression. Many examples prove the advantage of concentration. One manufacturer of several brands dropped all but one, and concentrated his entire advertising effort upon that one. In this way he built a business on a single article of four times the volume of his previous business on eight articles. Conversely it is true that most manufacturers who have successfully marketed one brand have been unsuccessful in trying to market additional brands later on.

A trade-name is practically the same as a trade-mark. Technically, the one is a name, the other is a mark, such as a seal or a pictorial figure, or some other design inseparably associated with the name and the product. But the same principles of law govern each. One important point of difference is that a trade-mark consisting of an emblem may be changed without detracting from good-will. Sometimes it is desirable to abandon a trade-mark; for instance, the picture of a woman may become so out of style that its continuation will make the product seem somewhat antiquated.

Modern advertisement at left. One of twenty years ago at lower right.
Notice how trade-mark now consists of new-coined name "Victrola" plus the old trade figure, the dog.

Sometimes an arrow, a triangle, an animal may be as strong a property right as a trade-name itself, when it has become definitely associated in the public mind with a certain kind of product. Like the steel framework in a skyscraper, the trade-name or trade-mark may be the skeleton on which the whole structure of public persuasion is built. Even a slogan like "it pours" in connection with Morton's Salt, "chases dirt" in connection with Old Dutch Cleanser, "most miles per dollar" in connection with Firestone Tires, "the universal car" in connection with the Ford—even slogans like these may form the spool on which the thread of persuasion is wound. But these slogans are too descriptive to be true trade-marks, and can seldom be protected

Copyright is often confused with "registration" of trade-marks. Registration under the Federal Trade-Mark Law applies only to trade-marks, trade-names, and kindred symbols. It means merely a public record that that particular trade-mark has been used and is spoken for. Copyright applies to pictures or manuscript, whether literary, commercial, dramatic, photographic, sculptural, informational, oratorical, poetic, topographical, technical, artistic, or what-not. Copyright has merely to do with granting exclusive privilege for the multiplying of copies of an original publication of any character.

In building a trade-mark, continuity of advertising is a prime essential. It is like rolling a barrel up a hill. If you stop, now and then, and let the barrel roll back to the bottom, you will make no progress. No matter how many hours you may spend altogether on pushing that barrel up the hill, if you do not keep at it you will ultimately be just where you started. So it is with making a trade-mark valuable. If you advertise like wild-fire for a month, and then drop it for a year, you will have to begin all over again; for, in the meantime, the public will have forgotten, and your trade-mark will be almost as little known as if you had never made that initial advertising expenditure.

CHAPTER IV

Analyzing the Problem

Whether a product be of local or national demand, whether it be advertised by retailer or manufacturer, there are certain basic elements which will largely determine how it ought to be presented:
What features of the product are worth talking about?
What qualities of the prospect can be appealed to?
What medium will be the best avenue through which to carry those features of the product to those qualities of the prospect?

We can answer these questions to a certain degree, if we can classify things to be advertised. In general we may say article No. 1 can be successfully advertised by "A" method, No. 2 by "B" method, and No. 3 by "C" method. (See chart page 28.)

In the first place, there are many things which must be advertised on a price basis, particularly in retail advertising. In such effort the aim, method, and result is to undersell the other fellow. Such advertising represents great bulk. It is the simplest form and open to so little variety in method that it is omitted from this general analysis of product and prospect.

Suppose you have to advertise something entirely new. Before knowing what to say, how to say it, whether to illustrate it, or where to place your "copy," you must know many things discoverable only by analysis of the product to be sold and of the prospect to whom you hope to sell. Of course, this will not decide all vital questions in regard to how, when, and where you should advertise; but, with the exception of the class of goods which must rely on cut-price for popularity, perhaps these three "pigeon-holes," A, B, C, may include almost anything which you may have to present to the public through publicity.

For instance, take the stock of a professional baseball club. Probably the first thought would be to use bulletin-boards, painted in nice "June" colors, to intensify the appeal of the ball park. But if you ask, "How much does the public know about this stock?" you will have to admit to yourself: "This is an investment proposition. It is not familiar to the average citizen. It is a new thing. Moreover, it is not actively wanted. It is in no way a necessity." Your task, then, is to make it known and wanted. To do that you have got to put your story where it can be read thoroughly. In other words, you could see at a glance that this "product"—this baseball stock—falls under the class of the "Unknown-Unwanted."

Knowing that, you will then have to analyze your prospective investor. What would be most likely to get his attention? Probably "novelty" would be the answer. Therefore, "FIRE THE UMPIRE IF YOU WANT TO" would be a telling head-line for one of your "ads." It would suggest the novelty of the investment. No matter how slight his interest might be, that kind of an appeal would suggest to any fan the idea that this stock would give him a part in the management of the home team. Then, how would you accomplish the next step—that of creating desire? Your proposition of itself ought to make him want a share or two —that is, if he knew something about it; so, if the medium used is suitable, description is the next essential. But, in addition to that, you must make Mr. Fan seek more information—or, in other words, allow you to talk to him personally.

That is to say, your advertising of an unknown—and unwanted—"product" like this should be expected to create enough desire to make the prospect seek more information, send in his inquiry, or be more receptive to the salesman who called. Such advertising should not be expected to pay for itself from direct sales resulting from the "ads."

Upper left—an announcement of twenty years ago.
The modern advertisement below is one of a series on "10-second filing."

This illustrates the value of analysis of product and prospect. In this case an investigation revealed that the average prospect sought speed in filing and finding letters. Note watch in man's hand.

There are three broad avenues through which you can influence people's decisions as to whether or not to purchase. These are:
1. Business (profitability).
2. Pleasure (pride, joy, etc.).
3. Weakness (fear, vanity, etc.).

Of these, business instinct is a considerable element, but it has to do with the logical mind, whereas pleasure and weakness have their source in the feeling; these two gates to susceptibility are, therefore, of easier access, and through them you can set into action certain processes stronger than the logical processes of the mind.

So you might appeal to your prospect's business instinct by showing how this baseball stock ought to pay big dividends. You might awaken his sense of pleasure by proving that it would be gratifying to be "among the first." You could suggest to the possible buyer how he would like to hear himself remark with pride: "I got a slice of the new baseball stock—did you buy any?" And you could appeal to his human weakness by giving the stock the atmosphere of a toy—something new which would tickle the boyish side of the grown-up "fan."

When your analysis of product and prospect has accordingly taught you these points, your problem simmers down to a choice of whether you should spend your money in newspaper, bill-board, street-car space, or otherwise. Of course, personal contact would be best, but it would be too expensive. Circular letters might be worth while, but their cost would be $20 or $30 per thousand of prospects reached, whereas the same sized space in a publication would cost 40 or 50 cents per thousand of people.

You know from analysis that your advertising has got to be of the "reason-why" persuasive variety—that it must be descriptive and persuasive, and that thoroughness of treatment is necessary. For this purpose any medium that is read-on-the-run is out of the question. Your advertisement must be put where the reader not only merely sees, but also

ANALYZING THE PROBLEM

looks and reads. Therefore, in "A," in the class of the "Unknown-Unwanted," it is necessary to use the newspaper or the magazine, or some other medium which is closely read. Unless you do put your advertising where it can both suggest and actually persuade, then you cannot hope to make known the unknown, and to make wanted that which is unwanted—unwanted both as to the specific brand and also as to the general class of which it is a part.

One distinguishing point in a product of this kind is its cost.

To make a woman buy "This" cake of soap instead of "That" (both being the same in price) requires just one result, *i. e.*:

1. That you make her desire to buy "This" instead of "That."

You do not have to persuade her to spend any money which she otherwise would not spend.

But the "Unknown-Unwanted" product is far from a necessity, to get her to buy this entails two tasks:

1. To make her spend money she otherwise would not spend.
2. To make her buy your particular brand of the thing for which you create a desire.

And even if your product is a necessity, still, if it costs more than other similar goods, you may have to use the same sort of persuasive advertising as on the products under "A," because, in the case of higher-priced products, whether they be necessities or luxuries, your task is twofold:

1. To make the consumer spend MORE than otherwise would be necessary.
2. To make her choose your brand above all others.

All new products and luxuries go into the pigeon-hole of the "Unknown-Unwanted." So do Cutex, Multigraph, Encyclopædia Britannica, and many others. For such must not only make known their names, but also they must establish the identity of the species to which they belong. They must prove whether they be fish, fowl, or flesh, and then they must show why the possible purchaser ought to have something of that species. Unless they monopolize their field they must also show why the public should prefer their particular brand above all other possible brands of the same type.

We now come to a class of products which lies in a middle-ground. They are neither known nor unknown, neither wanted nor unwanted, so let us call them the "Half-Known-and-Half-Wanted." For example, take a new automatic telephone. This is operated without operators. You turn a dial and get your number yourself. You have no one to abuse. You can be morally certain as to whether the party sought is really busy or not. Though it differs in many ways, after all it is a telephone, and, in that fact, is of fair familiarity. As to the demand for it, well, it's in the class of "Half-Wanted."

"You see, I subscribe to a manual phone system now, and to put in the automatic phone, also, would require the spending of more money than I really have to, and in a way might be an unjustifiable duplication." Something like that is the average attitude at first.

Thus, you would find that this product, on analysis, would fall under the head of the "Half-Known-and-Half-Wanted." It would be but semi-familiar and only passively desired, both as to the specific thing itself and also as to the class of goods of which it is a part. To win the prospect's attention, therefore, your aim should be to prove it a necessity. You must explain a great deal. You might, for instance, tell how it works. You might show why it works better than other things with which it competes. Only thereby can you create desire. To start the impulse to action in the prospect, you should prove the profitability of your article. You must make him feel he'd better have it after all.

Of the major human incentives, "business instinct" might be the best one to which to appeal when advertising this sort of product. The business instinct could be aroused in the case of the automatic phone, for instance, by showing how this service would save money. You could tickle the sense of pleasure of your prospective subscriber by getting him to feel: "Well, what's the use of my denying myself?" The next task would be to play upon his inherent weakness by making him feel: "Well, I'll have to get it eventually. I guess I might as well sign up for one now." And while appealing to his weakness, you might appeal to that most powerful of all his susceptibilities, fear, by suggesting how he might fall behind his rivals by not having an automatic phone in his store or office.

Thus, through an analysis of this second class of the "Half-Known-and-Half-Wanted," you can tell what features of the commodity to emphasize; which appeals will best bring about the necessary stages of (1) attention, (2) desire, and (3) action.

Therefore, in advertising products "Half-Known-and-Half-Wanted" your copy must be strong with display value, which will awaken a potential interest; it must also be persuasive with real reasons, designed to create desire; and you must use mediums that are more than merely glanced at, for the mere flaunting of a name, or a trade-mark, will never create desire for the "Half-Known-and-Half-Wanted." You must place this kind of advertising in publications which are read —the newspapers and the magazines.

The products which fall within this class are numerous; automobiles advertising, for instance, are among the most prominent. Here, too, you have usually to make the purchaser spend money which he otherwise would probably not spend, for such products are seldom necessities. To that extent this class is the same as the class of the "Unknown-and-Unwanted," and is different from the class "C," where the kind is really known and wanted, even though the specific commodity may be "Unknown as to Brand."

The main difference between the "Unknown-Unwanted" and the "Half-Known-and-Half-Wanted" types, is that in the latter class you do not need as much description to explain the idea of your product.

Yet, to make people buy the "Half-Known-and-Half-Wanted" commodity you must not only make them want the commodity in general—you must also make them want your specific brand. You must first establish a desire for something of the same kind as the thing which you advertise. But, since the desire is half-created to begin with, your main task is to make the specific thing which you advertise preferable to all others in this class.

Often a commodity, such as an automatic telephone, or an automobile, or a vacuum cleaner, or any patented device, may at first belong in the class of the "Unknown-Unwanted." As such it may necessitate the most complete description. Then, as the commodity becomes better known through advertising, it is automatically graduated from that class into the "Half-Known-and-Half-Wanted." Then, as something which is fairly well-known, it will require more and more emphasis as to its special brand rather than in regard to the general class of which it is a part.

Now we come to the class of the "Unknown-by-Brand." This name is deceptive, but is the only one that will distinguish this class of products from the two already discussed, as well as in regard to just what the advertising must do in this case. The title is deceptive because into this class go the army of names which have become practically a part of the nation's vocabulary. "Uneeda" Biscuit comes under this class, with "Sapolio" and all the other well-known cleaners.

Although "Unknown-by-Brand" may, therefore, appear a paradoxical name, it is used to suggest that the thing is not "Unwanted," and, that the sole object of the advertising is to change "Unknown-by-Brand" into "By-Brand, Well-Known." All products whose utility and general properties are utterly familiar, and which are actively wanted, fall under this heading. They require no educational work. They simply seek popularization, which repetition of name can provide. You don't have to tell the public that "Old Dutch" is a cleaner. You need not play up the advantages of scouring the steps in front of your home. In advertising such a brand, which is part of a species recognized as a necessity, your main task is to make the name of your particular kind so well-known that automatically the woman, on going into

ANALYZING THE PROBLEM

the store for something of that kind, will call for your special brand.

In other words, the element which you should emphasize in order to gain attention should be the name itself. You may build up its attention value as they originally did with Sapolio, by connecting it up with so many different things as to make the name each time enjoy the notice that novelty always elicits. And, where the chief task is the building up of a special brand of a needed commodity, you can create desire simply through repetition. You must drum the name in, time after time, until finally, by suggestion, you get the housewife to ask for your brand instinctively rather than for the one that your competitor has to sell.

You need not make the buyer spend money that she otherwise would not spend. You do not have to change her tendencies or convictions a great deal, in order to switch her over to your brand. To get action you must simply persuade the consumer to try your kind the next time she buys.

If you do succeed in getting her to try your brand, it is not so much through any appeal to her business instinct. The commercial profit to her in using your cleansing powder, for instance, instead of the other fellow's, is usually negligible. The pleasure element is her main point of susceptibility.

You might particularly appeal to her on the suggestion that it would be fun to try this new kind of yours. Thus her weakness would be your best point of attack. Your ammunition might be, for instance: "Eventually, why not now?" Your aim would be to make her say to herself: "What's the use of putting this off; I'll use this thing some day. I guess I will try it the next time I am at the grocer's."

Your main task in advertising products in this class is, therefore, to drive home the name. Argument is not necessary. In fact, some advertisers of this kind of product argue in this way: "If we gave reasons why, we would probably use our space in unprepossessing type-matter. If, instead of that, we use an eye-catching illustration, or an attention-compelling display of the name, then, with the same expenditure,

GENERAL ANALYSIS OF PRODUCT AND PROSPECT

(This chart is merely suggestive, and is not to be taken as a literal gauge for sizing up a product. Every product is surrounded by a different set of conditions, and, therefore, requires an individual analysis. This form may help, but its purpose is merely to set forth the idea and to stimulate advertising analysis.)

CLASS OF PRODUCT	LUXURIES or Products "Unknown-and-Unwanted"	HALF-NECESSITIES or Products "Half-Known-and-Half-Wanted"	NECESSITIES* Needed, but "Unknown as to Brand"
EXAMPLES	WASHING-MACHINES	AUTOMOBILES	CIGARETTES
How to Secure Prospect's	CLASS A	CLASS B	CLASS C
(1) Attention:	Suggest novelty.	Show necessity.	Emphasize name.
(2) Desire:	Describe virtues.	Explain details.	Repeat suggestion.
(3) Action:	Offer further information.	Prove its profitability.	Secure a trial purchase.
How to Appeal to Prospect's Susceptibilities	CLASS A	CLASS B	CLASS C
(1) Business:	Show how to make money.	Show how to save money.	Show it costs no more.
(2) Pleasure:	Invite to "Be one of first."	Suggest folly of self-denial.	Intimate that "It's fun to try it."
(3) Weakness:	Give it flavor of new toy.	Argue they'll "Get it eventually."	Inquire "Why not change?"
In Applying Above, What to Use by Way of	CLASS A	CLASS B	CLASS C
Copy:	Persuasive-advertising, plus description, plus reasons why.	Persuasive-advertising, plus reasons why and name-emphasis.	Name-Publicity—with display predominant.
Medium:	Mediums that are closely read—such as newspapers or magazines.	Mediums that are read—such as newspapers or magazines.	Mediums that are seen—almost any medium.

* Necessities which must sell for considerably more than average price come under Class A or Class B, rather than Class C, as they require the spending of more money than would otherwise be spent.

we can so much more effectively force our brand into the reader's consciousness."

In other words, "Name-Publicity" can be used for this class of goods. Suggestion can be accomplished through almost any medium—whether it be painted sign, street-car card, or poster. In fact, any kind of advertising, including magazine and newspaper, may be successfully used in this kind of endeavor to establish a specific brand. But even in such cases "Persuasive-Advertising" is usually better than mere "Name-Publicity," because it permits of adequate name display, plus copy which contains real interest and selling suggestion.

CHAPTER V

What Words Work Best on the Prospect

"Psychology" is a word that is often used in connection with advertising and selling. Usually it is loosely used. Sometimes it is the false weapon of the superficial, who seek to impress through the use of "highfalutin" terms. "Psychology" would not be used here at all, if it could be avoided, but it is necessary, not to impress or to mystify, but simply as a nickname for the briefest possible description of an important phase of advertising analysis. Psychology here means simply the analysis of mental processes, a study of how the human mind works; the word "mind" comprehends feeling as well as thought, for feelings, emotions, more frequently impel to action than purely intellectual processes.

"Copy" means advertising matter prepared for the mechanical processes of publication which precede its presentation in the newspaper, or magazine, or on signs, or wherever it is to appear. The word comes from newspaper parlance, in which news-writers refer to their writings as "copy," and in connection with advertisments "copy" bears the same relation as "MS." bears to a finished book.

The "Psychology of Copy" therefore means an analysis of advertising manuscript in its relation to the workings of the human mind and feelings. If you can analyze your prospects in the light of some such plan as that suggested in the previous chapter, you will know what phases of the human make-up to appeal to. You will, moreover, know what to emphasize, if you use a similar analysis to pick out the product's points of appeal.

"How to get these arguments into the prospect's mind through the avenues of least resistance," that is the next question. This need not be done in words alone. Some of the most expressive language of the day is that of newspaper cartoons; pictures, in fact, sometimes describe better than words. The general appearance of an advertisement alone is often eloquent. As the flaming red tie and checker-board suit on the gambler announce the manner of the man as clearly as if he wore a sign on his back saying: "I am a professional sport," so does the dignity of "Pierce-Arrow" advertising, through the atmosphere it lends, bespeak luxury, grace, elegance, and stability.

Need it be said that you should use language which your prospect can understand? We all know that; yet, the moment we hold our pen poised, ready to write a message to the public, we are tempted to use big words. Deep down we all in some degree resemble the proverbial colored parson, who impresses his flock with words of many syllables which his parishioners cannot understand. These words sometimes make a good general impression, and cause the flock to respect their leader as one who is learned and cannot be gainsaid. In certain cases long words may therefore be the very best kind of advertising—for the parson.. But in advertising you are confronted by one of the hardest obstacles that human nature offers: you must persuade people to spend money—to part with that which their toil has brought them. This you can only do with words they fully comprehend.

First of all, your prospects must understand what you are saying. How, otherwise, can you hope to budge them? You must more than persuade. You must inspire people to action—to the action of spending their money for your goods. Language suggestive of action is necessary. Certain principles to be applied in selecting words reveal themselves in the following comparison of two sentences: "Of momentous emolument to the populace of this metropolis, and environs, would it be to participate in our semi-annual merchandising event." Here, almost every word is sprung from Greek or Latin roots. "You can save money at this twice-a-year sale." This last sentence, whose superiority in effect is obvious, is made up of short familiar words. In the choice of words avoid adjectives whenever possible. After you have written an "ad," scrutinize all those words which qualify, and consider in each case: "Does this have to be an adjective? Can a verb express the same idea as well?" If so, you are lucky, because verbs swing the reader along, whereas adjectives are passive. For example, compare the effect of the verb "swing" with that of the adjective "passive" in the preceding sentence.

Study the style used by the leading writers of works that inspire, to learn what diction is the most effective in advertising.

Tricky writing will not do. A "cleverism" calls attention to itself and away from that which you seek to sell. It also detracts from sincerity. It is artificial. The sincerest and simplest copy is the strongest.

One prominent advertising man keeps a Bible in the top drawer of his desk, and turns to it frequently for ideas and for style. "The greatest advertising copy ever written," says another leading man in the profession, "is found in the public utterances of Abraham Lincoln, for he could make ten words do the work of one hundred—and he filled logic so full of warmth that it caught the heart as well as won the mind."

The best way to get to your reader through advertising "copy" is the simple way; that is, as a rule; for, although simple language is almost always best, there are a few exceptions when conditions may require different treatment. For instance, in the advertisement of something of exclusive class, when directed to a few who can understand polysyllabic words—people who buy for prestige rather than for businesslike reasons of price and quality—you may be better able to persuade if you use the superb elegance of lofty language and delicate indirection. But to the millions you must talk "turkey." And you must put what you say in terms that will not only reach their understanding, but their feelings.

What interests most people most? Their own personalities. A man is willing to hear about himself and his own interests all day long; but his ear soon tires if you tell him the story of your life.

"You," then, is perhaps the best word in the advertising

writer's vocabulary. Surely you can get a man's attention best with "you copy." You certainly can interest him best with what is called "you copy," and how can you convince him, and get him to act, if your persuasion is not of the "you" kind? But you can put this quality into your "copy" without ever using the word "you." All you need to do is to make your "copy" personal. Read any article or story in a successful magazine. Why does it grip you? Because it is talking about you; the hero's name may be Bill Brown, but you can see yourself in his place. He is a plumber, not a lawyer—but how like yourself he is. And those "Hints for Your Office"—how did that author know the conditions in your own business? Very little is said about the success of the magazine, for that would be "I" copy, not "You" copy.

There are different ways of putting the magnet of "You" into your advertising. One of these is by localization. For instance, when you see "United States" you don't feel that you are included. If you see the name of your State you are a little more interested. If you see the name of your locality you are still more interested. The mention of your own name, or of some peculiarity in connection with you or your circle, is what interests you most of all. So, if you live in Smithville, and an "ad" begins "Of the 1,800 Folk in Smithville," you are far more likely to read on than if the headline said "ATTENTION."

By localizing "copy," you can personalize it—personalize it in the second person, and so inject the "you" quality, even if you do not use that particular pronoun.

The most usual violation of this principle is where the merchant or manufacturer falls victim to the persuasion of some one who would write up his business. This gentleman forthwith plucks from his imagination some possible connection, either of name, historic association, or something of that kind, with which to link the name of Smith—his pro tem. employer. That done, he sets forth to glorify that incident with which he has coupled the name of Smith. He is thereby able to create flowers of eloquence in eulogy of the man who is paying for the "ad"; and the more this kind of an "ad" writer glorifies the man's business, the better pay he gets for his literary creation.

But where are the head and tail of this kind of "copy"? What is the aim? Does the manufacturer want to charge the cost of this advertising in with selling expense? Or does he want to put it down among the "incidentals" and justify it through the fact that his wife will be able to show it to her friends. If the "ad" is for selling purposes, why doesn't it tell people why they should buy of Smith? The few who care enough about Smith to enjoy such reading will buy from him anyway. It's the people who do not care whether your name is Smith or Perkins, but who will buy from you if they feel that you will give them better value, they are the ones whom you must address. Otherwise your advertising cannot be justified—at least, not on any basis of business.

As a great publisher has said: "Men are most interested in themselves, their possessions, their own wants or accomplishments. In business it is still largely meum—my factory, my wares, my styles, when I was established, my floor space, my thousands of employees. In good advertising it is consequently tuum—your wants, your wishes, your opportunity. Few women are interested in factories, process, or raw materials and machinery. Most women think from the counter out. In advertisements there should be more tuum and less meum."

Certainly there have been some advertising successes based on the "I" method; but that was when competition in advertising was not as keen as now. To launch the same product to-day with those same self-vaunting "ads" would be fatal to success. Yet there are manufacturers who honestly believe that the name of the manufacturer should be given first prominence in the display.

"Yes," we should reply to them, "we admit that your name is an asset, but your public knows who makes your product, and that knowledge in itself secures the maximum benefit that is possible from your name. In other words, that asset is conserved just as well, even if you don't give your name first prominence."

At right, an advertisement of 1900. Below, a modern page. (Note the prominence of tradename in the former.)

The "ad" at left is interesting, especially in its lack of name-emphasis. "The reason why some advertisers eliminate the logotype entirely is because every display of the name will have one of two effects on the reader: (a) The reader will see the name and assume that he knows all about the product. This reader is lost. (b) The reader may have a preconceived dislike for the product and upon seeing the name ahead of the message will pass on to the next page. This reader is also lost."

There are two great disadvantages against overemphasizing the manufacturer's name:

1. By giving the manufacturer's name as much emphasis as the name of the product, you have to promote two things instead of one. In other words, you complicate the name—and cut down the effectiveness of the message.
2. From the standpoint of results, the most successful advertising is the advertising which features the manufacturer least. This is not true of a store, but it is true of a product, because of the simple fact that the public is more interested in itself than it is in the manufacturer. The "first person" of the manufacturer is of little interest to the public.

Failure to realize this was evident in advertising of some years ago, which was based on some such theme as "Smith's Bread is Best." The public, without knowing it, thought: "Of course, Smith thinks his bread is best—but with so many other breads in the world, it can't be the best, and Smith must be just lying a little bit." In other words, that kind of advertising was neither interesting nor plausible; therefore it lacked the quality of persuasion.

To dominate a piece of copy with the maker's name eliminates the possible intrigue of that copy, and so weakens its chance of interesting the consumer. On seeing an advertisement plastered over with "Smith," the reaction is likely to be: "Oh! there is another ad of Smith, the Baker. I will pass on to something else."

On the other hand, upon seeing an advertisement that is designed in the interest of the reader rather than that of the manufacturer, the reaction is more likely to be something like: "Here is a nice-looking little lad. He seems to be healthy, and reminds me in a way of my sister's boy. He is eating bread and jam, and it says there: 'It's supper-time.' You know, that's a good idea. I have often told Minnie not to let her child eat pork and beans, when the best food is good bread and jam—and Smith's bread is certainly good."

WHAT WORDS WORK BEST ON THE PROSPECT 37

In either case, if the eye looks at an "ad," it will see what is advertised, whether the name takes up half the "ad" or only a tenth part of it. And if the "ad" is designed upon lines of interest and persuasion, the eye is likely to get something out of it besides the mere name of the product.

Of course, sometimes, when the name of the manufacturer is also the name of the thing, like Heinz Pickles or Ford Cars, the manufacturer's name cannot be suppressed.

And yet there is this interesting fact about a famous soap, named after its manufacturer, which is advertised in women's magazines: The manufacturer thought the name of the soap should have greater prominence in the full-page advertisements. These were designed to persuade the reader in favor of this soap, and also to get her to send in a few cents for a sample. To settle the argument, one of the magazines agreed to run its edition of a certain month in two divisions. In the first, the "ad" was printed with a large name-plate. In the second, the trade-name was printed ever so much smaller. The result was that the "ads" with the smaller name-plate "outpulled" the others four to one. Why? Because there was four times less "you" quality in the copy that was plastered so prominently with the "I" of the manufacturer.

Above all else, copy should be human. This fact has been expressed by that most human master of persuasion, Abraham Lincoln, who said:

"If you would win a man to your cause, first convince him that you are his sincere friend. Therein is a drop of honey that catches his heart, which, say what he will, is the greatest highroad to his reason, and which, when once gained, you will find but little trouble in convincing his judgment of the justice of your cause, if, indeed, that cause really be a just one. On the contrary, assume to dictate to his judgment, or to command his action, or to mark him as one to be shunned or despised, and he will retreat within himself, close all the avenues to his head and heart; and though your cause be naked truth itself, transformed to the heaviest lance, harder than steel and sharper than steel can be made, and though you throw it with more than herculean force and precision, you shall be no more able to pierce him than to penetrate the hard shell of a tortoise with a rye straw. Such is man, and so must he be understood by those who would lead him, even to his own interests."

CHAPTER VI

Suggestion—The Motive Power of Advertising

"Men should be taught as though you taught them not": that, from Alexander Pope, is the golden principle of advertising. In other words, advertising copy gains potency from an emotional rather than from a logical quality—its best weapon is example, not precept—its method is suggestion rather than instruction. Suggestion is the basis of successful advertising. And what is suggestion? As defined by the psychologist it is the imparting of " an idea or emotion leading direct to favorable action." In fact, it is the art of getting the other person to tell himself.

Although the mechanics of suggestion are fairly simple, the art of suggestion is among the most difficult of arts. Suggestion is possible because the mind inclines to believe every idea, unless it is contradicted. The ideas that enter the mind through suggestion are uncontradicted, and are, therefore, more fully persuasive.

But to understand how to use suggestion, the mind must be considered as if divided into two main parts:

1. The logical mind (the intellect).
2. The feeling mind (the imagination).

The intellect works in logical processes. It is the judicial department of the mind. It picks flaws. It weighs one thing against another. It disbelieves until persuaded by sheer force of logic and cold fact. Argument, the logical brand of argument, in the form of brief or in citation of authority, is the one process by which the intellect may be captured.

But the intellect is not much worth winning; its influence upon the question of what a person shall purchase is slight.

Almost everything we buy appeals rather to our imaginative mind, or our instinctive mind. Possibly some purchasing agents, possibly some engineers, now and then some business men, may buy as a result of the conclusions which have been reached in their logical minds through the cold consideration of facts. But in nine cases out of ten, the average person, the consumer, buys largely through instinct, largely through feeling; in other words, the buying impulse is almost entirely actuated by the feeling mind, or the imagination, as we shall call it, rather than by the intellect. Cold argument, therefore, seldom sells goods. The appeal must reach the imagination. That is why suggestion rather than instruction, example rather than precept, concrete picture rather than abstract generalization, are the things of which good advertising is made.

The brain is supplied by five sources, the five senses—hearing, feeling, smelling, seeing, tasting. Of these, all except "hearing," automatically work by means of suggestion. (Under hearing we include reading, because reading is only another form of hearing.) When we physically *feel* a thing, we tell ourselves about that thing. Our conclusions register in our intellect and our imagination through suggestion; and feeling is believing. When we smell a thing, we also find that our main mental stimulus is by way of suggestion; and smelling is believing. When we see a thing, it is the same way; and seeing is believing. And when we taste a thing, we throw up no contradiction against that sense. And tasting is believing. But to hear is not to believe, and to read is not to believe.

Therefore when we hear or when we read, that which comes into our minds is second-hand experience; it is not our own experience. The sentinels of our mind seek to contradict everything that would enter there through the spoken word or the printed page. But if what we hear or what we read is surcharged with things we can feel or smell or see or taste, then we are more likely to believe, more likely to be persuaded, because then the message enters our "feeling" mind, or our imagination, and it is less likely to be contra-

At top left, an advertisement of twenty years ago. It simply asserts—and makes superlative claims. How much more persuasive is the modern advertisement below!

The above "ad" sells through serving—its persuasion is based on helping young women to find careers. It seems to emphasize employment, but, by indirection, it builds good-will for the machine.

dicted, more likely to carry persuasion because it has registered upon the buying motives.

But the great question is how to achieve suggestion. In advertising there are these three principal ways of harnessing this great force:

1. By appearance.
2. By demonstration.
3. By diction.

Consideration of the value of "appearance" brings us face to face with the fact that Impression is nine-tenths of persuasion. How does the advertisement look when you first glance at it? What is its personality? Does it suggest the motive that will make you buy? If it seeks to sell fishing-tackle, does it make you feel the lure of the trout stream? Does it suggest value? Does it suggest quality? Is it clean-looking and inviting?

In considering the value of "demonstration" we find that the picturing of a product in the proper way achieves considerable persuasion. Of course, the visible object itself would do better, but the very illustration of it also suggests, and, therefore, persuades. And when we present this object at work, we tend to increase its power of suggestion, which helps to make the reader tell himself what you wish him to believe. Take a washing-machine. In itself it is a clumsy-looking piece of machinery. Picture it at work, and the woman can hear the swish of the water, can smell the soapy cleanliness, can almost feel and see the crisp, clean, laundered clothes as they come off the line.

An illustration may be definitely suggestive in depicting an act which you wish the reader to imitate. For instance, down near the coupon you may put the picture of a hand holding a fountain-pen, or you may illustrate a hand with a pair of shears, apparently in the act of clipping the coupon. One principle is that the human mind will obey by imitation any suggested act, unless it checks itself. It is this fact which makes such illustrations persuasive.

But through the method of "demonstration" we have cer-

SUGGESTION—THE MOTIVE POWER OF ADVERTISING

tain ways of using suggestion, other than those that act through word and picture. Actual demonstration, showing an object at work, is not only potent in attracting the human eye, but also in persuading. Sampling is based upon this principle, since it clearly enables the prospect to convince herself; and when the sampling takes the form of tasting, it may reach perhaps the highest point of persuasiveness through suggestion.

But the chief medium of advertising is language. It is by diction that suggestion can be made to play its most important part. The selection and phrasing of words so as to create desire is the highest art in the function of advertising. In the main, advertising words should paint pictures; they should touch emotional chords; they should play upon the feelings. Advertising words should aim at the imagination through the avenues of sight, smell, taste, and sensation; and if the subject is a product that is to please the ear, such as a talking-machine, the diction should appeal to the hearing, or should carry the suggestion of the human voice or the chiming bell, or the whispering violin. To choose the "*concrete*" is probably the main secret in achieving a diction that vibrates with persuasive suggestion. The human mind can conceive no pictures made of generalities, but it can visualize that which has shape or taste or weight or sound. Suggestive diction has more power in the message that it registers on the mind. It is also a tonic to attention. It is entertaining. It requires less effort on the part of the reader, for it puts into operation fewer mental processes. It transmits its meaning direct to the imagination, or the emotional part of the brain, without encountering the judicial scrutiny of the intellect or logical mind. To achieve Suggestion, you must choose specific words, instead of general words. A general word includes a number of ideas; a specific word names one idea. A general word names a class of objects; a specific word singles out from the class an individual. It is interesting to the public to know that you offer sail-boats made of "hardwood," but your prospect could picture your product more definitely if you used the word "mahogany."

Suggestion is also achieved by the use of figurative words. These are words used suggestively rather than in their literal sense. Instead of saying: "The finish of this car shines bright for years," suppose we say: "Its mirror-like finish will hold its youth indefinitely." Isn't the second choice of words somewhat stronger? "Bright" is literal; we all understand it. "Mirror-like" tells how the car looks. Everybody has seen a shining automobile, but it is striking to compare it to a looking-glass. And instead of its lasting "for years," to say it has "youth" is to remind the reader of human strength and grace. The words "mirror-like" and "youth" are not used to say precisely what they mean, but to suggest resemblances.

Comparisons, when used to carry suggestion, are known as "figures of speech." Comparisons between objects of the same kind do not involve figures of speech, such, for example, as: "This street is more beautiful than that"; "This water tastes like well water"; "Foch was as great a general as Joffre." They suggest nothing, they are literal, they are merely comparisons. But if these comparisons indicated points of similarity between objects of different kinds, then they would be either "similes" or "metaphors." The "simile" is more direct and usually demands the use of the word "like" or "as." For instance, if you say, "This will make your ice-cream as smooth as velvet," your figure of speech is called a "simile." It definitely and explicitly points out a resemblance. If we make the comparison so indirect that the reader must infer the resemblance, we call such a figure of speech "metaphor." For instance, it is metaphorical to say: "These electric lamps are a balm to the eyes." A metaphor spreads the meaning of the name of one thing over the name of another thing—by implication.

Another way of making a thought specific and concrete, instead of general, is through "metonymy." By this figure of speech we substitute one thing for another which the mind automatically associates with it. For instance, when we say "The screen is more eloquent than the pulpit," we mean that moving-pictures are more convincing than verbal sermons.

SUGGESTION—THE MOTIVE POWER OF ADVERTISING 45

But we automatically associate "screen" with the movies, and we automatically associate "pulpit" with sermons, so we can carry over our suggestion and picture our thought in terms of the concrete and the specific.

Possibly the most common method of carrying suggestion is through the figure of speech known as "personification." Personification usually includes "metaphor," or "metonymy," or both. It is called "personification" when it gives personality to things that are not persons. For example, a motortruck is called "The big brother of the railroads"—a soap is personified by the slogan, "Have you a little Fairy in your home?"—a cleaning powder is personified by the head-line, "Let the Gold Dust Twins do your work."

There are other varieties of the figure of speech, but they are mostly adaptations of these three fundamental forms which are described above, *i. e.:*

1. Similes and metaphors.
2. Metonymy.
3. Personification.

All such figures of speech are strong, or weak, in proportion to their naturalness. The simplest and most natural figures carry the strongest mental pictures. When a picture is far-fetched, the reader is more apt to think of its cleverness than to conceive the picture which the figure seeks to convey. Figures that are built on common experience are the ones that breathe life and give force to our thoughts.

Suggestion is also dependent upon the general structure of our advertising copy. There are four general plans for building an advertisement. These are:

1. Narration.
2. Description.
3. Exposition.
4. Argument.

Of course, the story form is probably the most alluring and has the greatest power of suggestion. The incident is the basis of good narration. We all see things happen that we remember and tell about. The method that we use in narrating these incidents is the best method for the use of narration in advertising. In our narration we may frequently stop the active course of our story and begin to describe something. For instance, we may say: "At that moment, the chimes of a neighboring church began to peal forth the tune of 'Nearer, my God, to Thee.' He stopped the roadster. The man and the woman raised their eyes and saw the saintly spire as it towered against the clouds with a white cross atop its pinnacle like a lily flower on a slender stem."

Descriptions of this kind usually enrich narration, particularly if the description "paints a picture," even though it be merely one of words. But to clarify description, you must make sure of your perspective. A description should always have a definite point of view. In the above description (which, by the way, is somewhat extravagant, in order to emphasize the method) the point of view is from the seat of the automobile, where sit the two persons who are the subject of the narration. Of course, description is more frequently used by itself, not as part of a narration.

Exposition is the usual method of explaining a thing. For instance, according to this method we tell how a safety-razor works. If you described how the safety-razor was invented, that would be a narration. If you described the parts of the safety-razor and its general appearance, that would be description. But when you explain the use of the article, that is exposition. In other words, description tells how a thing looks, whereas exposition sets forth the meaning of a thing, or explains the use of it.

Argument is probably the least effective method in advertising, because it usually appeals to the intellect rather than the imagination, and it is therefore susceptible to antagonism and to contradiction. Argument should seldom, if ever, be used in advertising, as it is likely to be devoid of suggestion, and, therefore, lacking in persuasiveness.

CHAPTER VII

Ways to Win Attention

The easiest approach, then, to your prospect's mind and heart is through an appeal to his interest. But before you can reach your possible customer with this appeal, you must make him read, or at least see, what you have to say.

The element that will enable you to attract his attention is Display. It is probably the most important single factor in all advertising, because no advertising succeeds unless it gets attention.

Display is of two kinds:

1. *Eye-Display.*—The mechanical kind that simply catches the physical eye regardless of any action of the reader's mind.

2. *Mind-Display.*—The psychological kind, which wins attention through the fact that it calls forth some active mental interest in the prospect's mind or feelings.

There are, in general, six different ways in which Eye-Display may be accomplished:

 1. Contrast.
 2. Beauty.
 3. Illustration.
 4. Color.
 5. Size.
 6. Motion.

Contrast may consist of an eye-compelling, attractive border, or any number of eye arresters, such as an unusual shape. Take, for example, a want-ad page in a newspaper observed from a distance. Doesn't it seem gray and flat? Now take a little "ad" in the centre of that page. Rule it off with heavy black lines an eighth of an inch thick. The box-border will make that one-inch ad stand out so strongly that it will have as much display value as would an ordinary "ad" of many times its size. Contrast is what does it.

Or, Eye-Display can be accomplished through other means of contrast. For instance, suppose you surround your message with white space. This lack of typography in the vicinity of your advertisement is so unusual that it will also catch the eye. Thus it will possess Eye-Display value of high power. You often see this method used with great effect—but if every one used big splashes of white space, it would be of little value—because it would lose the quality of contrast.

Sometimes Eye-Display may be achieved through sheer beauty. But this must be more than negative beauty, because the average eye is not sensitive to æsthetic values. The element of beauty must be more than pleasing if it is to win attention. It must also have force—force enough to draw the eye and grip the attention, and so will probably involve the use of an illustration.

The illustration certainly stands first and foremost as an instrument of attraction, either for the eye or the mind. The world's first language was made up of pictures; and the human eye and mind still continue to prefer illustrations to mere reading matter.

Two other big elements in Eye-Display are Color and Size, both of which have a certain influence on the intensity of any message.

Color attracts—this is an axiom of nature. There is a color-hunger in every eye; an advertisement in colors is sought out. Then, too, colored advertisements are unusual, and enjoy, in that respect, a contrast with the bulk of black-and-white advertising. But even if a certain magazine carried ninety-nine advertisements in color and only one in black-and-white, the ones in color would still be worth considerably more—and would pull better—just as they do to-day.

So, also, with size—size itself achieves Eye-Display. Just as a great redwood-tree, or a whale, commands more than usual attention—so large size is a tremendous element in the Eye-Display of advertising. Motion has a like power. In mechanical display signs, where motion can be an element, the attention value is many times what it is in similar signs which have no moving features.

But Eye-Display, although it may be the most important of all elements, must not be emphasized to the sacrifice of favorable impression. Often the far-fetched use of a repulsive display combination may spoil the power of the advertisement. And Beauty, or, at least, freedom from repellent ugliness, is necessary.

"Good appearance" is a plank that every advertiser should have in his working platform. When you are tempted to combine a screaming yellow with a flaming red, resist. Don't ruin the persuasive ability of your work simply in order to make your "ad" attract more eyes. *Favorable* attention is the only kind worth striving for.

Good Eye-Display should not only increase the attention-getting quality of an "ad," but should also supplement its ability to create desire in favor of that which it advertises. Even where the rules of color harmony are not violated, even in the plain black-and-white, we see many violations of the principles of Eye-Display. Usually, these errors result from an effort to make the attention-getting part of the advertising so heavy with black ink that it repels more than it attracts.

Excessive contrast is as dangerous as color-discord, for, though it may not actually repel, it will at least keep the reader's attention from pleasantly sauntering over your message. The eye is sensitive. It does not like to be hit too hard. Therefore, the Eye-Display that attracts in a simple way, with taste and in harmony, is the most effective.

Distinguished from the merely physical display, or Eye-Display, is the other form of attention-getting, which we will call "Mind-Display." This attracts the mind. It is subtle, and far less mechanical than Eye-Display, but the same mechanical means which make for Eye-Display may also be used to effect Mind-Display.

Instead of working through the few physical laws of optics, Mind-Display must deal with the complex and less definite laws of the mental processes; for Mind-Display is more a matter of Psychology. It must fit in with the mechanics of the brain and feelings, if it is to succeed. Take, for instance, the kind of Mind-Display which prompts us to sympathize. This wins our interest and attention through the fact that it strikes a common chord in our make-up.

Suppose, then, that we can associate that which we seek to sell with some cause in which our prospective purchasers have a keen interest. Imagine, for example, that we are advertising a certain product while our country is at war. If we can carry in our display a suggestion of love for the flag, a hatred for the foe, and if, at the same time, we can logically weave into that suggestion a persuasive argument in favor of our product, then we shall win a quicker attention and a keener interest than we could possibly win without achieving this association of ideas. Fusion of ideas is the basis of this system of getting attention. It merely means the linking-up of your appeal with something which of itself has a certain interest.

There are many instances of this kind of Fusion. For instance, during the Mexican turmoil, when Americans were intent upon it, the Fairbanks Company came out with: "If we must clean up Mexico, why not let the Gold Dust Twins do it?" This clever soap manufacturer virtually appropriated for his own washing-powder an interest which the Mexican disturbance had created.

There is another means of fusing ideas which helps persuade the mind as well as attract the eye, by putting the product into a novel relationship with some atmosphere which, of itself, pleases the prospect. For example, certain candy manufacturers, during the hot summer months, found it profitable to picture a box of their chocolates on the snowy bank of an ice-clad river. Some cracker people also made a success with a similar idea—they portrayed their box of biscuits frozen into the centre of a cake of ice.

But, sometimes, there are accidental instances in which a fusion of ideas works against favorable Mind-Display. Suppose you are advertising a food. If your "ad" is placed next to an announcement showing the picture of a tombstone, you are justified in resenting it; for Mind-Display which associates your food with a cemetery casts an atmosphere of gloom around your product. On the other hand, a certain "ad" sought to gain Mind-Display through the element of timeliness. The copy was published the first week in October and mentioned October in the head-line. The publisher usually published a calendar of the current month in every issue, so he placed this October "ad" right below the calendar of October. One might have thought that the calendar was part of the "ad" and had been paid for by the advertiser.

If you connect your product with some interest which already holds the reader's sympathy, then your product will unconsciously receive some of the kindly feeling which goes out toward the associated idea. That is why it is always best to make your illustrations present such people as the reader is likely to admire. For instance, if you are advertising a soda-fountain drink, it is better to give a picture of beautiful débutantes sipping the beverage at some palatial drug-store than to portray a group of dirty, barefooted brats guzzling at some dilapidated fruit-stand on the street corner. As far as argument goes, the enjoyment of the urchin may theoretically be as strong as the pleasure that those young ladies experience; but people do not think much of the street arab's taste, whereas the finely dressed girl is supposed to be an epicure.

Harmful Mind-Display results from unfortunate Fusion of Ideas. For instance, suppose you use the picture of a monkey as a trade-mark in connection with high-grade food products. No one can see that animal, so usually vile with vermin, without disgust. And this disgust cannot help but be carried over into the reader's judgment of the food.

The Mind-Display which commands the most favorable attention and best effects persuasion usually suggests an associated idea which carries admiration or, at least, approval. Of course, there may be exceptions to this—particularly where so-called negative "copy" is necessary. In this case, where you have to use fear in order to bring about a sale, it may be desirable to fill your Mind-Display with a fusion of ideas with something despicable. For instance, in advertising a liniment for rheumatism, the best kind of Mind-Display might be the repulsive figure of a used-up man, with limbs all gnarled and twisted.

But pleasant suggestion can generally be used to best effect in connection with Mind-Display. The face of the charming nurse calling attention to San-Tox products is dainty enough to suggest the quality and refinement of the pharmaceutical products which she adorns. Or recall the bewhiskered face of the kindly old doctor who looks at you, his eyes flashing with the sparkle of health; that keen look, plus the words, "He don't use coffee," suggests volumes of persuasion, and, above all else, accomplishes the first task of winning the reader's eye. Such is a combination of Eye-Display with Mind-Display.

The element of repetition is likewise accomplished through Mind-Display. In fact, for that purpose Mind-Display is supremely important. Some of the nationally advertised articles were once financial failures. With most of them the first years showed a balance on the wrong side of the ledger, but the men who then lost sleep wondering how they could meet their advertising bills are mostly millionaires to-day. The little element of cumulative result through repetition has been the key-note to these successes. This "rolling snowball" process, by which the effects of an advertising campaign keep piling up, depends on repetition. For instance, suppose H-O Oatmeal had changed its name to "Sweet Oats" after the first year, and then, after that, to "Oatlets," and after that to something else. Suppose the first year they used a Dutch Girl as the keystone of their advertising. Suppose that the second year they used a soaring eagle as their trademark. Such suppositions are foolish, but the point is this: If H-O had not stuck to a certain trade-mark, would H-O be the factor that it is in the cereal market of to-day?

Any sensible man knows that H-O and all the rest of the big successes that advertising has created have been built on repetition. It may not be repetition of one argument. It may not be repetition of trade-mark. It is probably repeti-

The twenty-year-old "ad" at right illustrates the danger of negative appeal. The mind tends to confuse the lens with a disagreeable graveyard. The modern "ad" above, in the words of advertising manager, Hugh A. Smith, "is one of the best and most effective advertisements we have yet done, basing that judgment not only upon our own opinion but particularly on the reaction obtained from the magazine reading public and our own trade. We believe it to be of the most general interest, more impressive in its message and on a distinctly higher plane than any previous campaign of ours."

54 A SHORT COURSE IN ADVERTISING

tion of different elements of Mind-Display, which, at a glance, have continually caused the readers to say: "I have heard about that product before."

If the atmosphere of your advertising is continuously uniform, and if the Mind-Display of this week's "ad" enjoys a favorable harmony with the Mind-Display of the "ads" that have gone before, there is likely to be a repetitive value, insuring a cumulative result, which brings the total of advertising benefit to a point far in excess of the sum of the separate benefits of the individual "ads."

But continuity can be carried too far, and while there should be a continuous *note* of Mind-Display running all the way through, the advertisements should be sufficiently different in size and in style and in theme to escape monotony; for that which the public sees all the time it does not see at all—at least not with *awakened* attention.

Repetition of Mind-Display is most evident in department-store advertising. The principal reason a store does a business this year far and above last year (which in turn showed bigger volume than the year before) is the cumulative effect of its service and its advertising. Most department-store "ads" could be identified by the public, even if they were not signed. Their atmosphere would tell the tale. Their Mind-Display would suggest so many previous "ads" that the reader would almost feel that this was So-and-So's announcement.

That continuity of Mind-Display is what brings cumulative results out of the repetition of advertising. It not only works for the local institution—it also makes national successes more successful. In the case of E & W collars the simple repetition of name, with one or two clean-cut arguments, has won. Few know the arguments for E & W collars, but the mere name, in connection with those Mind-Displays of distinctive trade-mark and distinguished appearance, talks to you almost every day—to-day in the whisper of very small space, to-morrow in the thunder of the quarter page, until the E & W has become embedded in the public mind as an admirable institution.

CHAPTER VIII

How Do Size and Color Aid Display?

Your advertising must be seen. How can you be sure on that point? Will you make it big? Perhaps the most elusive question in the consideration of advertising "copy" is the problem of size. Sometimes an "ad" may be one-fourth the size of another, and, therefore, cost one-fourth as much, and yet "pull" just as efficiently. Certainly, four small "ads" will often pull better than one large one. At other times you spend your money on small space, to find that an advertisement twice as large will pay better than two of the smaller "ads."

If display-value alone is your aim, other elements than sheer bigness may be used for the same effect with less cost. For instance, when color is available, it sometimes takes the place of size. A red spot as big as a dime in the centre of a newspaper page would win as many eyes as an ordinary black-and-white space one hundred times as large; but, from a practical standpoint, color cannot be bought in any medium without buying maximum size as well. Colored advertising, in magazines, for instance, is practically limited to the full page as a minimum.

Color is a science in itself. There are three qualities which every color possesses, namely:

1. VALUE.—*Vividness*—the quality of salience—contrast between light and dark—*i. e.*, black-and-white as against gray.
2. HUE.—*The color-quality*—the degree of difference possessed by one color as against others—*i. e.*, red as against green.
3. CHROMA.—*The comparative degree of "hue"*—the vividness of a color as compared with its normal—*i. e.*, scarlet as against maroon.

56   A SHORT COURSE IN ADVERTISING

For an ordinary understanding of advertising, you need not know a great deal about the mechanics of color. The fundamental question is that of attention-value. The main colors in the order of values are red, black, green, orange, blue, purple, and yellow. Certain combinations, such as black and orange, or red and white, are especially strong. In fact, black may sometimes be stronger than red, especially if the surrounding color is predominantly red. For instance, on a booklet with a cover of pink stock, black will have a far higher attention-value than red.

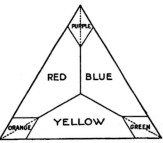

There are only three primary colors—red, blue, and yellow, as shown in the accompanying chart. From these, other colors can be made. Three of these colors, called "secondary" colors, are shown at the corners of the triangle. Each of these three secondary colors is made by combining the two primary colors which are next to each other at that point. For instance, yellow and blue make green of different shades, depending upon the proportions of the two primary colors, yellow and blue. The primary colors red and blue make purple, violet, and other colors; while the primary colors red and yellow make orange, etc.

In addition to their attention-value, colors have certain powers of suggestion. As G. G. Addington has said:

"Each color lends a certain atmosphere. The predominating atmosphere of blue is cleanliness. Red suggests heat, excitement, power, force. Green is cooling, soothing, and in most tones restful to the eye. Yellow is an appetizing color to the general mind, so experiments show.

"The shades and tints of these colors carry the same general atmosphere, unless through some unfortunate mistake one should choose one of those sickening shades of green, or a washed-out red or blue.

"The pastel shades, dainty tints we see most often in the advertising of toiletries and silks, conduct to the reader's mind

HOW DO SIZE AND COLOR AID DISPLAY? 57

an alluring picture of feminine charm. In the advertising of 'Lux' this idea is brought out clearly, the general tone being light and graceful, a soft blending of pastel tints. Here, too, blue predominates in most cases, for cleanliness is a feature. The advertising of 'Djer Kiss' toilet preparations makes use of the 'beauty appeal' of pastels to good advantage.

"You wouldn't choose, however, a background of pastel tints for an advertisement of 5-ton trucks, for pastels are lacking in brute force. It takes solid shades to put across the idea of strength and stamina. The attributes of the article advertised should 'harmonize' with the color used; just as surely as it is necessary to choose the proper type face to tell your story of power or daintiness or beauty."

Just as the more colorful the "ad," the more it will attract the eye—so the larger you make your "ad," the more attention it will command. And the smaller the comparative size of competing factors, the greater the attention-value of a given "ad." For instance, on a page made up of "ads" averaging ten and fifteen inches in size, a six-inch "ad" will have less chance than if it were on a page with "ads" which did not so overshadow it.

In most mediums, the size of an "ad" decides itself. For instance, the largest posters (called 24 sheets) must be 8 feet 10 inches by 20 feet, no more, no less. The 3-sheet poster must be just 42 inches by 84 inches.

In car cards, the standard size is 11 inches by 21 inches. But even in posters and car cards, where sizes are standard, there is a constant effort to startle and dominate through abnormal bigness. Every now and then some advertiser tries to get two car cards together, so as to make his message twice as big as that of any one else. Even in the case of the large 24-sheet posters, Chesterfield's Cigarettes were displayed with two and even three of these alongside of each other, so as to make this advertisement, in three parts, occupy a length of almost 60 feet.

But in publications there is almost no limit to the minimum or maximum size of advertisements. In newspapers

58   A SHORT COURSE IN ADVERTISING

there have been advertisements occupying 36 pages, as in the case of a Western department store when opening its new building, which took an entire section of a Sunday newspaper. And yet in that same newspaper there was an advertisement 2 inches wide by less than ¼ inch deep; and in those magazines which are so-called class or trade publications, inserts of 16 pages devoted to one advertiser have not been uncommon. Even in national magazines 4-page "ads" have been used; but in mediums of this kind the double-page spread is the usual example of sheer size. Frequently this is bought in color, as, for example, the advertisements of the Willys-Overland Automobiles; and sometimes it is bought with color on one of the two pages of the double spread, with black-and-white on the other, a method employed by the Goodyear Tire Company. But the usual unit of space in publication advertising is the full page; for a full page in color secures just about the next maximum of possible attention-value.

Considerations other than that of attention-value and of adequacy of space to permit of a persuasive message sometimes influence the question of size. A great deal of advertising is done with one eye on the consumer, and the other eye on the trade—on the dealers who almost control the destiny of any product. To make a dealer feel that a product is forcibly advertised, you must usually impress him with the bigness of the space that you are using. Size, too, depends upon what your competitors are doing. If other manufacturers in your line are using full pages, you had better use *at least* full pages, or stay out of the publications they are in; otherwise, you will give a confused impression that you are not as strong as they. In other words, if you whisper with ⅛ pages, while in the same issue your competitor is shouting with full pages, the comparison is bad for you.

As a rule, however, maximum space is best merely at the start, in order to force distribution by impressing the trade, and to compel attention by startling the public to a knowledge of your new product through the "shock" or "drive" method. Then, after distribution is achieved and the public begins to know that there is such a thing on the market as

HOW DO SIZE AND COLOR AID DISPLAY? 59

that which you advertise, ½ pages, or possibly less, may be more profitable than full pages or double pages.

As a general rule, however, any advertisement ought to aim to dominate the page. If there is no other advertisement on the page, a 2-column by 4-inch "ad" may be adequate, from the standpoint of visibility, impressiveness, and persuasiveness; but when, as is usual, there are several "ads" on a page, the advertisement which is ⅓-page size is likely to approximate the golden mean.

Size is frequently determined by the amount of money available, and this is sometimes a false guide, because the advertiser frequently thinks that he has got to use all the publications in which he is asked to buy space. Often it is better to use large space in a certain publication, or in a group of publications which pretty completely cover your market, and to stay out of the other publications entirely.

The average national publication of a million or more has a tremendous "coverage," when you consider that less than 10% of the families of the country have aggregate incomes of $3,000 or more per year. On that estimate less than 3,000,000 families are very good prospects. A national circulation of a million is likely to reach a big proportion of this desirable class. Larger space in one of these publications is, therefore, more effective than smaller space in several of them. A publication's circulation should be regarded as an audience—a given group of people to whom you are trying to carry conviction. If you speak to them for a half-minute, and then run down the street to another audience and speak to them for a half-minute, you will not get nearly as many converts as if you spent sufficient time in really convincing one of those audiences.

Not only is concentration of big space in fewer mediums a principle toward which advertising experience has been tending, but there is also a tendency to conserve space by omitting advertising for certain seasons of the year, and then concentrating the advertising in large quantities during certain limited periods. This method of concentrating advertising during, for instance, two months in the spring and two months in the fall, is what is known as the "drive" system. It corresponds to the military methods developed by the Great War, based on the principle that a concerted, concentrated attack over a specific area, in a specific time, will gain more ground than the same expenditure of men, munitions, and effort applied to a continuous push day in and day out.

The problem of "How large should an 'ad' be?" is one of the most discussed in advertising. There are examples where successes have been made on very small space, and these examples are always the arguments of those who advocate minimum size. But there are two answers to this argument: The first is that these successes would possibly have been greater if larger space had been used, and the second is that for every one example of advertising success built on small space you can point to a thousand examples built on big space.

It is logical that dominant size is usually best, for these three reasons:

1. VISIBILITY: An "ad" twice as large as another is more than twice as likely to be seen; and visibility increases with size in almost geometrical progression.
2. IMPRESSIVENESS: An "ad" twice the size of another, through the mere fact of its size, has more than double the power of creating a favorable impression, which tends to build prestige and good-will in the minds of all who glance at the copy, even if they merely read the name of the product.
3. PERSUASIVENESS: An "ad" twice the size of another permits of enough space to carry the right kind of display, illustration, and text; therefore, it has more than twice the chance to convince and to persuade.

In seeking to find an answer to the question, "What size should an 'ad' be?" many experiments have been made. These have tended to contradictory conclusions. Some tests would prove that a full page is four times as effective as a half page, and a half page is three times as effective as a quarter page. But such proof is fallacious. In fact, there have never been enough cases to establish any laws. These

HOW DO SIZE AND COLOR AID DISPLAY? 61

experiments are made on the basis of a few advertisements. The experimenter asks a man to look through a magazine and see what "ads" he can remember. Then he has other men do the same thing. It is found, after adding up the results, that the readers recall four times as many full-page advertisements as they do half-page advertisements. But, alas, so many confusing factors enter into such a test that the conclusions cannot be regarded as final. For instance, a man may remember a full-page advertisement of Williams's Soap because that is the kind which he, himself, uses. If he recalls a Williams's Soap "ad," that doesn't mean that he remembered it solely on account of the fact that it occupied a certain space.

No one can ever fix upon a law that will determine all questions of size; but you can determine approximately how big a space you should use for a certain kind of an article under certain conditions. By experiment, you can answer a specific problem conclusively.

Size of space depends on the kind of a product you advertise and upon specific merchandising conditions. For instance, if your product attracts a voluntary interest on the part of the reader, so that people look for your "ad" and read it of their own accord, you do not need as much space as if you had to attract involuntary attention—as if you had to force your prospect to read.

If you advertise a cream separator in an agricultural publication, you will enjoy a voluntary interest, because people in the market for that kind of a thing will probably, of their own accord, look through the advertising pages of that publication for some sort of a cream separator. They will therefore look for your "ad" with a purposeful attention, a voluntary interest. But if you advertise an aeroplane, you will probably find very few of the readers who are in the market for such a luxury. Practically no one will look purposely for a product such as your "ad" presents. To force attention, therefore, you will have to shout louder. Consequently, you will have to use bigger space.

Take an example less far-fetched than an aeroplane. Suppose you have to advertise some soap. Nobody says:

"Where's this week's *Journal*—I want to see if there are any soap advertisements in it." Yet, Mr. Farmer frequently says: "Where's this week's *Journal*—I want to see if there are any cream-separator advertisements in it." So, if you are to get attention for your soap, you will have to work for it, and in order to create that unwilling interest, you must talk through fairly large space.

It is often true that the more nearly universal the possible demand for a thing, the less voluntary is the interest toward it—usually, common commodities are faced with an involuntary or unwilling interest on the part of the advertisement's audience, perhaps because things of universal need are usually made by so many different manufacturers that they are continually and widely advertised. For instance, take the case of cleaning powders. They are advertised very heavily. By virtue of that fact, readers become used to cleaning powder "ads." When they do pay attention to them, it is not because of their will, but because the power of the copy compels their interest in spite of their apathy.

Luckily, articles of universal demand are susceptible to so great a sale that the expenditure necessary for increased size of space is warranted. But, on the other hand, if the demand is limited and specific, as, for instance, in case of rubber roofing, you cannot afford to use such big space, since so small a percentage of your readers are usually in the market for that thing at a particular time; nor do you need such big space, since those readers who are earnestly in search of rubber roofing will seek out such advertising anyway. They will entertain toward it a voluntary rather than an involuntary interest, and you will therefore get their attention even if your space may be small.

But regardless of the kind of product, the tendency is toward large space, as is shown by these figures covering a whole year in one of the world's greatest magazines:

> Quarter pages were used 374 times.
> Half pages were used 274 times.
> Full pages were used 772 times.

HOW DO SIZE AND COLOR AID DISPLAY?

Of these full pages, over half of them were in color.

Seventy per cent of the entire advertising space was in full-page units.

The advertisement which is disguised as regular news matter strategically enjoys the voluntary interest that a reader naturally applies to the kind of news matter which such an "ad" imitates. This steals attention, even though it has neither contrast, novelty, nor great size. In so far as this "reader" advertisement looks like news matter, which it is not, in so far it wins attention. This tricks the reader into a voluntary interest. And in the long run this style loses because such trickiness shakes the reader's faith and prevents conviction.

CHAPTER IX

Printing Processes, Plates, and Papers

The three main printing processes generally used in the advertising business are:

1. The "letter-press" or "type-printing-press" process, in which the engravings and type to be printed are raised.
2. Lithography, in which process the matter to be printed is not raised, but the impression is secured by the reaction of water and grease on a lithographic stone.
3. The "web" or "rotary" press process, in which the paper is printed from a roll and the form is electrotyped or stereotyped and curved to fit a cylinder.

The method of the usual letter-press process is to press the metal type or plate against the paper—the same principle as that of pressing a rubber-stamp against paper. The printing "form" (which comprises the type in combination with the plates) is left flat, and is pressed flat against the paper.

In the "type-printing" process the original engraving is a half-tone, zinc etching, or wood-cut. The half-tone and zinc can be printed directly on paper, but it is necessary to make a duplicate or electrotype of the wood-cut.

Type printing is made on several different kinds of presses, according to the size and quantity of work to be done. For a small job a "job" or "platten" press is used. If the quantity is very large, or the job of sufficient size, duplicates or electrotypes are made and the job printed on a "cylinder" press, in which case the paper is carried around a cylinder in single sheets and comes in contact with the flat face of the type and engraving.

On long runs, especially in big newspapers, the web or

rotary process is used. In this the original flat metal form is transferred to a cylindrical metal mould by the stereotyping method. The printing is then done from this rounded form, instead of from a flat form.

For reproducing a piece of advertising by the hundreds of thousands—especially color work—lithography is the most economical method to use. As the term "litho" suggests, this implies the use of a stone. The original engraving for lithography is an unusually fine stone, the best specimen of which is obtained from Bavaria. The design is engraved or drawn on this stone, and then duplicated or "transferred" to another larger stone or sheet of zinc or aluminum. This large stone or metal sheet is the printing plate or "transfer" from which the paper gets its impression. Lithographic stones are of a peculiar composition. By keeping the stone wet during the printing process all of its surface, except that which has been etched (by the transfer of picture and type), keeps damp and thereby repels the oily ink. Consequently, when the ink roller passes over the stone, only those parts of its surface which are to make an impression on the paper take any of the ink.

Lithography is the cheapest process for printing labels and such small multicolored pieces of printed matter which must be produced by the million. In these cases, one big stone often contains dozens of reproductions of the design. From this a great sheet can be printed in one impression. This one sheet, when cut up, will furnish a hundred or more labels.

If you will look at a proof of a piece of lithography you will notice little crosses here and there. These are called the register marks. They are intended to enable the pressman to make sure that the colors, each one of which is put on in a separate printing, fit accurately into the intended design— or, as the printers say, "register" properly. For instance, in poor lithography, the side view of a human face will bear a flesh color which does not quite reach the edge of the profile on one side but laps over beyond the outline of the face and into the hair on the other side. This is what comes from inaccurate "registering" of the plates or stones.

Three types of machines are used in lithographic printing. The original lithographic printing-press is called a "flat-bed" or "stone" press. Here the large stone "transfer" is used, and the paper comes in direct contact with the stone. This is a slow-operating press and has been, to a great extent, replaced by more modern machines. It is still well adapted for display work in which heavy cardboard is used.

The second style of machine is called a "direct" or "rotary" lithographic press. Here the metal printing plate or "transfer" is fastened on a cylinder, and this metal plate comes in direct contact with the paper. This style of press is used in printing large color editions, particularly labels.

The third type of press is known as the "offset" press. Here the sheet of zinc or aluminum (to which has been transferred the required number of designs) is attached about a cylinder which comes in contact with a rubber blanket. This rubber blanket is on a second cylinder, and comes in contact with the paper on a third cylinder, leaving the inked impression on the paper. This "offsetting" of the design is what distinguishes the press. The offset process makes possible the use of rough papers to take the most detailed half-tones, because the rubber blanket sinks its impression into the surface of the paper, no matter how rough, whereas the half-tone plate itself, not being pliable, impresses its likeness only on the high spots or upstanding parts of the rough surface.

Recent developments have given prominence to the photogravure process, which is described by S. T. Leigh, the Australian authority, as follows:

"The Intaglio process of printing, which had been known in America by many names such as 'Gravure,' 'Rotogravure,' and 'Photogravure,' is that method of printing wherein the design is either carved or etched below the surface of the plate or cylinder of copper.

"Although it has no connection with lithographic printing, it is the direct opposite of the common forms of newspaper and magazine printing, in which the subjects are either etched or raised in relief from the surrounding surface. In Intaglio printing the design is etched in with acid through the medium

PRINTING PROCESSES, PLATES, AND PAPERS 67

of a sheet of sensitized gelatine (known as carbon or carbon tissue).

"On web rotary perfecting presses for Intaglio work for newspaper supplements the form consists of a steel cylinder with a coating of copper about three-sixteenths of an inch thick. The cylinder must be perfectly true, smooth, and highly polished. Reversed positive photographic films are laid in their respective places in the cylinder, and designs are etched into the copper surface with acid solutions. The cylinder revolves through a tray of ink when put on the press, coming out dripping with ink. A thin steel blade the length of the form, known as the 'doctor,' oscillates across the surface of the plate, scraping all the superfluous ink from the cylinder, leaving the surface clean, the ink remaining only in the etched or sunken parts of the cylinder. The paper passes between the copper cylinder and an impression cylinder driven by friction, having a medium-hard rubber surface. The impression cylinder forces the paper into the etched parts, and the ink is then deposited upon the paper. Because of the varying depths of the etched impressions, different thicknesses of ink are deposited on the different tones. This causes some difficulty upon the solid tones. After the sheet is printed upon one side it passes into a heated box or around a steam cylinder, when heat is applied to the printed side to dry the ink; from here it passes to the second impression and is printed upon the other blank side. It again passes through the heat oven, where the ink is again dried, and from here it goes through the "former," and is delivered in folded sheets.

"The copper-faced cylinder upon which the design is etched is either drawn or deposited copper of the purest quality. After the printed issue is finished, following any printing run, it is placed in a grinding machine, where the etchings are removed, and after having again been polished it is ready for another etching.

"Artistically, Intaglio printing has advantages over any other, as the film of ink deposited upon a solid is thicker than in the medium tones or high lights. It presents a soft, velvety appearance, soft tints, delicate shadings, and lifelike brilliancy of detail, which distinguishes it sharply from any other process."

Original printing plates are of three general kinds:

        1. Half-tones.
        2. Zinc etchings.
        3. Wood-cuts.

These printing plates, or engravings, are indiscriminately referred to as "cuts," whether they be half-tones or zinc etchings, or what-not.

Half-tone engravings are the most common. They look like photographs. They must be made either from photographs or from wash-drawings, and their greatest value is in photographic reproduction.

A half-tone is so called because it not only prints solid black-and-white (such as ordinary type matter contains), but also intermediate tones between black-and-white—in other words, grays. The half-tone reproduces any shade of gray as well as black-and-white. In that way it accomplishes photographic reproduction.

You can readily understand how a black impression can be made on a sheet of paper, and how *not* printing anything on certain portions of white paper will leave a white space. But how does the half-tone, with the same metal surface, print black here and gray right above?

The half-tone is made from a sensitized plate. A screen is put between this sensitized plate, which is in the camera, and the "copy"—which is either a photograph or a wash-drawing.

This screen is simply a piece of glass divided by many diagonal lines running from upper left to lower right. These lines are intersected by a similar set of lines running from lower left to upper right. They divide the screen into little diamond-shaped "islands." In other words, the lines hide from the sensitized plate, corresponding lines on the copy. And they expose to the sensitized plate the little parts of the "copy" which "peek" through the little open "islands" between the intersecting lines of this screen which stands between the plate and the picture.

Which has the greater appeal—the picture of the baby in the modern "ad" above, or the photo of a man in the twenty-year-old "ad" at the right? There is no question on that point. And it is just as obvious that "Mennen's Talcum" is a better handle for the public demand than "Mennen's Borated Talcum Toilet Powder."

Thus the clear spaces, or "islands," between the intersecting lines, reach the sensitized plate and thereon record themselves. If you look at a half-tone through a microscope, you will see that it is made up of thousands of little "pimple-like" islands, or bumps, and thousands of little valleys, dug out from the surface. These little valleys correspond to the lines of that screen which was interposed between the copy and the sensitized plate during the exposure.

For the sake of visualization, just suppose that these little bumps on the plate are mountains, and the little lines are depressions which we may call valleys. Here, for instance, is a spot on the plate which will reproduce the black hair of a man's head. At this point the little "valleys" are very, very narrow, and the tops of the little "mountains" are stubby and broad.

Over yonder there is a part which is to reproduce the light gray of an overcoat. Here we find that the open spaces, or "valleys," are wider, and the tops of the mountains are proportionately thinner. It is these "mountain tops" which touch the paper. If these are thin they leave but a little spot of ink. If they are thick they leave a big spot of ink. The latter, of course, makes a darker impression than the former. In this way half-tones permit of variations in the shades of grays and blacks.

Half-tones and, in fact, all engraving plates, are "blocked" or "unblocked," according to whether or not there is a wooden base to which the metal face is tacked. This wooden base is of sufficient thickness to make the printing surface exactly as high as the ordinary type. Sometimes a solid lead backing is used instead of a wooden base.

"Tooling" of plates is the cutting away of metal on the printing surface of a plate—or the correction of defects by hand-engraving after the photo-engraving is finished.

Half-tones are divided into three main divisions, according to the way in which they are finished:

1. Square half-tones—if they are simple square-cornered, like an ordinary photograph.

PRINTING PROCESSES, PLATES, AND PAPERS 71

2. Silhouette half-tones—if they are "outlined"—if the superfluous background is cut away so that it reproduces a blank white.
3. Vignette half-tones—if the background immediately surrounding the objects gradually fades off from a clear impression into haziness, and finally into nothing.

Half-tones are also divided as to screens—in other words, as to coarseness or fineness. This "screen" refers to those parallel lines which ran diagonally across the "screen" which was originally placed between the copy and the sensitized plate at the time the negative was taken. In a coarse half-tone these lines may be so far apart that there are sixty of them (in the form of "dots") to an inch. When the dots are closer the half-tone is finer. They may be so close that two hundred of them, side by side, will measure only an inch in width.

The coarse-screen half-tone of about "60-screen" is the only kind that is usually feasible for the ordinary newspaper, because the surface of the newspaper is often so uneven that a "fine" half-tone, a 100-screen or finer, would blur and blot. On smooth-surfaced paper, such as that used in magazines and some books, the half-tone of about 133-screen is the best.

The zinc etching is the simplest form of engraving. This is like a half-tone, except that in the "zinc" no "screen" is used between the copy and the sensitized metal plate when the likeness is being photo-engraved thereon. This sensitized plate, like a photographic film, records the image or "copy," which, in the case of a "zinc," is simply black-and-white—such as crayon-drawing, or black pen-and-ink on white. Such art-work, in general, is classed as "line-drawing."

Since the "zinc" etching has no screen like the half-tone, the zinc cannot reproduce photographs. Yet the very smallest black-and-white type matter, for instance, can be minutely reproduced on a zinc etching.

If a photographic subject has to be put into a zinc engraving, then the "copy" must first be changed into the plain black-and-white by being made over into a pen-and-ink or line-drawing. Naturally, plain zinc etchings are, as a rule, the best kind for newspaper use, because they do not have to depend upon the smoothness of the printing stock for faithful impressions. And to further insure an unsmudged result, the larger "white" spaces on the plate are cut away entirely. This elimination of that part of the metal surface which is *not* to print is called "routing."

If you want either an unusually sharp reproduction, or one which is obviously different, you may use a "wood-cut"— particularly if the subject to be treated is an engine, or some other mechanical work. Wood-cuts are quite like zinc etchings, except that they are of wood instead of metal. They have to be carved by hand rather than etched out by acid. The original wood-cut, itself, is seldom used; duplicates are made from the original pattern plate. So, when it comes to the final printing, the wood-cut's likeness is put on the paper through the intermediary of an etched metal, which is simply a duplicate of the wood engraving.

"Electrotypes" are also included under the general vernacular of "cuts." They are neither original half-tones nor zinc etchings. They are simply "carbon copies," as it were —simply duplicates. These "electros," as they are usually called, are made by taking a wax impression of the original printing plate, whether a half-tone or zinc. Through a chemical process the resultant wax mould becomes surfaced with a shell of copper. This shell of copper is then stiffened by being backed with lead. The result is a complete electrotype. The deeper the copper shell, the better the electrotype.

You can readily tell an electrotype from the zinc pattern plate, from the fact that the former has a copper face instead of a white-metal surface. You can readily tell an electrotype duplicate from an original copper half-tone pattern plate, by the fact that although both of them have a copper face, the electro has lead-like metal beneath its copper face—whereas the half-tone is copper clear through to the block on which it is fastened.

PRINTING PROCESSES, PLATES, AND PAPERS 73

When it is necessary quickly to duplicate type matter and plates, such as are used in the newspapers, the stereotype process is used. This means that a blotter-like substance, called a matrix, is pressed down on the surface of the metal type form (which combines composition and cuts). As a consequence, a reverse impression is made on this blotter-like substance—the "matrix." Lead is then poured over this matrix. The result is a metal plate, which, of course, conforms to its blotter-like mould (the matrix), for the matrix is simply an impression taken from the original type form. The lead thus cast in this matrix mould becomes a "stereotype." This is a solid plate. Its face is an absolute duplicate of the original composition and cuts.

Stereotypes are used in newspapers because the printing speed necessarily demands a rotary press, and stereotypes are easily made in cylindrical form. It is impossible to use an assembled form of individual type and plates on a press revolving as fast as a newspaper requires. No matter how well locked together such might be, they would fly apart when running at the rate of speed necessary for publication. That is why it is necessary to make each page into one big metal semicylinder by the stereotype process.

The question of what paper stock is to be used is important, in case it is a printing job. You will undoubtedly have before you a full sample case, showing the different styles available. These little samples indicate in what size they are carried in stock and also the weight. The quotation is usually on the basis of a ream, which is generally 500 sheets, and the weight usually means the number of pounds that each ream weighs. Printing papers usually come in sheets of 24 x 36, 25 x 38, 26 x 40, 28 x 42, 32 x 44, or 36 x 48 inches.

There are hundreds of different kinds of papers from which to choose and hundreds of different kinds of colors. You will have to select largely on the basis of the feeling and the looks. The grades of paper vary from the cheapest newspaper stock, made of wood-pulp, to the finest linen bonds, made from selected rags.

Nearly all of the better papers are "sized." In other

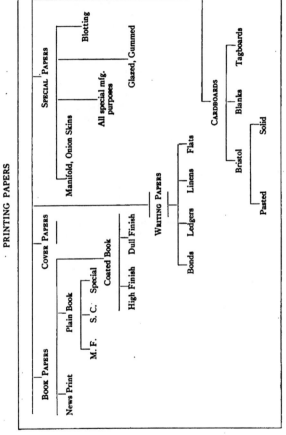

This chart shows a few of the classifications of the most frequently used printing papers. (Chart evolved by Robert Paviour, of Alling Cory Paper Company.)

words, they have been treated with either a vegetable or animal substance, which fills up the pores of the surface of the paper so that the ink will stay on the exterior, and not soak into the body of the stock. The best agent for this sizing is animal glue. Clay is sometimes used as a filler to bring about a smooth surface.

Paper varies in the quality of the sizing used. It also varies in another big point—"calendering." Calendering means the ironing of the paper between heavy rollers. The usual surface obtained in this way is called "machine finish," sometimes termed "M. F." If treated with a little better care, it is sometimes called supercalendered. When it is supercalendered as well as sized, the paper is called "S. & S. C."—meaning "sized and supercalendered."

But even this paper may not have a sufficiently glossy surface. Therefore, your particular job may require an "enamelled" stock, with its surface artificially finished with a coating of starch-like material known as china clay. This can be finished with a dull effect, or a shiny brilliance.

There are many hundred special kinds of papers, including the rough antique and other dull finishes which lack gloss. Also, there are scores of different kinds of stocks designed particularly for use as covers on booklets. Beyond these there are the many bristol-boards or cardboards, for signs, mailing-cards, tickets, etc. "Boards" of this kind usually come in sizes 22 x 28 inches.

These boards are built of different layers of paper and each layer is called a "ply." Thus, if a stock is said to be six-ply, it means that it is six layers of paper thick. When "point" is used to designate thickness of stock, it does not mean the same unit of measurement as the "point" in type. A lithographic board of 125 point, for instance, would be only a fraction of an inch thick.

CHAPTER X

Type and Typographical Arrangement

Suppose you run your advertisement across three columns, a width of over six inches. Your first temptation will be to make each reading line run straight across those three columns. You may think that such a three-column line will impress more strongly than three one-column lines. As a matter of fact, your line of three-column width will be hard to read, unless the type is of a certain size, with a certain amount of white space between each line.

This matter of legibility is one of the first factors in the success of an advertisement. If the "ad" cannot be read it is useless. Anything that reduces legibility is bad—bad not only because of difficulty in reading, but also because it detracts from good appearance. For instance, a heavy black display in reading matter usually results in an illegible smear, and an ugly effect which repels rather than attracts, for the human eye is sensitive and fastidious.

Then, too, a thoughtless concentration upon size and emphasis may tempt you to employ only capital letters. Such typography also prevents easy reading. You can readily see the logic of this. The human eye is used to reading the news in a newspaper. The usual news column is a little over two inches wide. It is made up almost entirely of small letters—not capitals. When, therefore, you force an eye to travel over all capitals—a style of type entirely different from that to which it is so accustomed—the eye is likely to revolt.

Experiments in psychological laboratories prove that the eye can best grasp the type which is of "upper and lower case" (that is, of capital and small letters, used according to the accepted rules). Also, these experiments prove that the eye cannot grasp more than four "units" at one time. So, in head-lines, where each word is virtually a "unit," the cap-

TYPE AND TYPOGRAPHICAL ARRANGEMENT

tion which comprises only four words has more chance than the caption of many words.

When within an "ad" you use large type to attract attention to some special point, this use of display will be effective in proportion to the infrequency with which you resort to it. Italics are better for this purpose than all-capital letters, or mere blackness; yet italics are hard to read, because they are unnatural. Italics are likely to interfere with the even running of the reading eye. If you wish to emphasize a certain word or set of words, the better way is to underscore, when that is possible.

In the news column (on which the human eye has been largely "brought up") you will find little or no emphasis, either by way of capitals, or italics, or underscoring. The eye is not educated to word-emphasis, except through the medium of the personal letter. When you seek to emphasize in handwriting, you use the underscoring method. As a result this method has become the natural and, therefore, the best method by which to accomplish internal emphasis, when internal emphasis is necessary.

The selection of type is very important, because, as the expert, Benjamin Sherbow, says: "Printed matter must be more than readable—it must be easy to read."

There are almost as many different kinds of type as there have been leaders in the art of printing. In general, types may be divided into four main classes:

1. Old Style—Types such as Caslon, the style used in the reading matter in the usual newspaper.
2. Modern—Newer faces of type, but based on the original Roman faces.
3. Gothic—Square-cornered, ugly, plain faces, such as are usually associated with old circus-posters or cheap bargains.
4. Text—Fancy faces, such as "Old English" type, usually used on formal announcements or memorials.

In each of these families there are many "relatives," each with a different name. Although the general families differ decidedly, the varieties within a family are similar, and you need not burden your mind with their names. You can usually have a type book at hand for reference, so that you can select the kind you want.

The technical word that describes a given class of type is "font." Each font has a different character of "face," the term which designates the printing surface of types. For instance, a Cheltenham font is a certain branch of the Old Style classification, but there are different tribes of Cheltenham. One is Cheltenham "condensed"; in this the letters are abnormally narrow. If you wish a Cheltenham type which is abnormally wide, you will ask for Cheltenham "extended." Then there is the Cheltenham italic, the kind of Cheltenham whose component types slant from lower left to upper right. "Bold" specifies the style of face which makes a heavy impression, and this is sometimes called "black face." It is the opposite of the light-face type, whose printing surface is sharp and thin, and whose impression is dainty.

While the Gothic family is rugged, plainer, and simpler, you can employ the Old Style, achieve strength and boldness, and yet have the graceful curves and other little points of attraction which distinguish the old-style and the modern faces from the blunter Gothic.

Type varies in size from that which is so small that it is called "pearl," up to that which is so large that it has to be carved out of wood, because in metal it would be too heavy to handle.

You hear printers say: "That's 8-point—that is too small —it ought to be 12-point." What do they mean by "point"? A point is merely an arbitrary measurement which equals 1/72 of an inch. When you want to use type an inch high you specify 72-point. If you want your reading matter of letters 1/6 of an inch high, you indicate 12-point. There is some type as small as 5-point—smaller, therefore, than a fourteenth of an inch high.

A point, then, is a technical term to designate the height of type. The width of a unit of type naturally varies. The letter I, of course, is narrower than the letter W. Luckily

TYPE AND TYPOGRAPHICAL ARRANGEMENT

the letter M is just as wide as it is high. Out of this coincidence grows the fact that the unit for measuring width is called an "em." The "em" of any certain height of normal type is the width of the letter M in that particular size. And the "em" is as wide in number of points as that particular type happens to be high. For the "em" is as wide as a given type's height. Thus, the "em," in connection with the 12-point type, is 12 points wide. Since in this case the unit of measurement is 12 points (or 1/6 of an inch), there are 6 "ems" in each inch of width, and so a column 2 inches wide comprises 12 ems. Likewise, the em in a style of type 36 points high is 36 points, or ½-inch wide—and so on.

"Better make this a 12-em column," you will sometimes hear the printer say, without regard to the size of the type to be used—whether it be 12 points high, or 18 points, or some other height. When used independently in this way the em refers to a "pica" em, which is always a 12-point type. So, even if you do not know what the height of type is to be, a 12-em width means 2 inches wide, whenever such specification is made without regard to height of type; and the term "em" is usually used in this loose way, and means a 12-point unit of width.

"Line" is another arbitrary term of measurement. Most space is sold on the basis of this unit. The "line" is technically an agate line. This is theoretically 5½ points high. In other words, there are 14 of these lines to an inch, so that in a publication where the space is quoted at 10 cents a line, $1.40 is the price for each inch of height in a given column. But if such lines of type are set "well-leaded," they will occupy more than 1 inch for each 14 lines, because "leaded" means that little lead partitions separate each line from the one above it. "Set with 2-point lead" means that between each line you want a strip of lead (2 points, or 1/36 of an inch thick). But, if you do not want the lines of type "opened up" or spread out in this way, you ask that they be set "solid." This means that the bottom of one type rests on top of the type in the line below, with no space between the two lines except the slight one caused by the fact that the base of the type is larger than the surface from which the impression is taken.

In getting type set, you have the choice of three main methods:

1. Hand composition.
2. Linotype.
3. Monotype.

Hand composition is the manual, or "hand-set" method. This permits of the greatest possible variety in type composition. It is the most flexible way of setting any display matter or any text.

Straight reading matter can be set more economically by machine. In the ordinary running type of the news columns most newspapers use linotype. By this method each line of type is set in one solid piece of metal as wide as the width of the columns. Necessarily, then, if an error is made the entire line must be thrown away and a new one "cast" in its place.

With the monotype machine each individual letter is made into a new type, freshly cast for that purpose. This machine uses a roll of paper similar to that used for the automatic player-piano, in which a special machine—similar to a typewriter—pricks a series of little holes. When this roll is applied to another machine, the caster, there results the individual manufacture of a particular unit of type, whether letter, punctuation mark, or figure. Virtually, then, the monotype makes type to order in the sequence necessary, and automatically sets up the type as needed.

The best way to learn the typographical fundamentals of advertising is to visit a printing-plant and a lithographing-plant. If you absorb simply the main facts you will then have enough of a working basis to instruct your printer intelligently.

The average printer, left to himself, is more likely to seek the fancy result than to produce maximum effectiveness, from an advertising standpoint, so you can secure better advertising if you specify to the printer what you want, in

TYPE AND TYPOGRAPHICAL ARRANGEMENT 81

a general way at least. The usual way to do this is by means of a "dummy," as it is called, if you are working on a booklet or circular, or anything with extensive text; or by means of a "layout," if it be an advertisement to be reproduced in magazine or newspaper.

The "dummy" is simply a rough plan suggesting what you desire. If you want a booklet, you should give the printer a dummy suggesting the stock to be used, the number of pages, and the design of each page. This "dummy" should show the size and kind of binding you require. It should indicate, by a rough sketch, where the illustrations are to go. As to the reading matter, you will figure out how many words, of the size of type which you want, can fit into a square inch. From this you can calculate how much matter will go on each "type" page.

Here are tables showing the amount of space that certain sizes of type take, both in square inches and in number of lines:

Approximate Number of Words in Square Inch	Approximate Number of Words Per Column Inch (Column 2¼ Inches Wide)
6 point leaded.........34 words.	6 point leaded.........73 words.
6 point solid..........47 words.	6 point solid..........101 words.
7 point leaded.........27 words.	7 point leaded.........58 words.
7 point solid..........38 words.	7 point solid..........82 words.
8 point leaded.........23 words.	8 point leaded.........49 words.
8 point solid..........32 words.	8 point solid..........69 words.
10 point leaded........16 words.	10 point leaded........34 words.
10 point solid.........21 words.	10 point solid.........45 words.
11 point leaded........14 words.	11 point leaded........30 words.
11 point solid.........17 words.	11 point solid.........36 words.
12 point leaded........11 words.	12 point leaded........23 words.
12 point solid.........14 words.	12 point solid.........30 words.

(Leaded means 2-point leads.)

A "type" page is that part of a full page which is to be covered with type or illustration. If your dummy has a page 6 x 9 inches, outside measurement, and an inch-wide border or margin of white space all the way around, then your "type" page will be 4 x 7 inches.

When possible, you should paste into your "dummy" proofs of the cuts you propose to use. Under each of these you should indicate any wording you wish to use as captions to describe the cuts. You should also designate what the head-lines should be, writing them in on the dummy itself. As to the reading matter, you simply need to make clear where it is to go, without attempting to embody this text in your "dummy." The manuscript, generally separate and in typewritten form, is attached to the "dummy."

The same points apply to the usual "layout." If for a newspaper or magazine, your layout should be practically a "map" of the way you want the illustrations and type matter arranged. Any big head-lines should be sketched in on this "map." If possible, you should either paste in a proof of the cuts, or if you have the cuts handy you should ink them over with an ordinary rubber-stamp pad, and hammer their impression directly on the layout, right from the printing plates. The reading matter should simply be attached to the layout with each part of the manuscript marked so as to show just where each paragraph is to be inserted in the composition as laid out.

These layouts and dummies correspond to blue-prints and specifications in the field of building. They are architectural instructions by which printers, engravers, and artists build the final structure.

Usually the front of a building—the façade—is that which makes a building beautiful or not beautiful. A building that looks well at first glance has a great asset simply in its appearance. This is true of advertisements, too; if they are good-looking they have won half the battle.

The general composition of an advertisement decides whether or not it is attractive. The very best art work is not worth its cost if the general design is not harmonious—if the different parts of the advertisement do not fit together in a way that insures both attractiveness and the proper presentation of the selling message.

There are three main factors in securing this result:

    1. Proper emphasis.
    2. Unity.
    3. Simplicity.

Although this "ad" has few words, it is really full of reason-why persuasion, because the picture itself is a demonstration of the product.

The general skeleton of an advertisement, or of a page, should be built according to that law of proportions which involves what is known as the "golden section"—the ideal proportion that sculptors and artists have adhered to throughout the ages. The golden section means that the weight is so balanced that the optical centre of the composition is slightly above the actual centre of the advertisement or page. This ideal centre, for most pleasing effects, is two-fifths the distance from the top and three-fifths the distance from the bottom.

Proper emphasis requires the subordination of everything else to one dominant factor—the factor which requires the greatest display. To try to emphasize several factors in a layout is fatal, for then, in the finished product, the component members will compete against each other for the attention of the reading eye.

Unity requires that an advertisement or a layout should hang together, that all component members should be well knit, that they should be so related and joined to one another that the entire advertisement or page will itself form a unit—at least, from an optical standpoint. Unity may be gained through illustrations—by carrying the illustrations in an "L" shape or in an "S" shape, or some other form that will tend to make the eye comprehend the advertisement as a single object; or unity may be achieved by the proper use of white margins; or it may be based on the proper arrangement of type.

Simplicity requires that the advertisement be kept free from "gingerbread"—from all the fancy uses of type and illustration and arrangement which tend in themselves to engage the eye and so divert attention from the advertising message. And yet, the type should be distinctive, for without this quality it is of little interest. But distinctiveness may be gained by the skilful arrangement of type rather than by the use of novel faces. In fact, Caslon type—the old, old standby—may be arranged to constitute a most distinctive piece of typography, although it is simple and readable.

Type can be used to suggest the quality of the product

which it advertises. Certain styles of dainty light-faced type suggest the pretty whiteness of silk wedding-dresses. Rugged faces, such as Scotch Bodoni, suggest the solidity and strength of a great bank. Other faces of type suggest novelty, some suggest speed, some suggest jollity, and some suggest cheapness.

The surroundings affect type as much as shrubbery, lawns, and trees affect the appearance of a home. The setting with which to surround type may be an illustration, or may be white space. White space is a very important factor in the building of any advertisement or page. White margins should be in certain proportion to the size of the page and to the amount of reading matter on the page, and each white margin should bear a certain proportion to every other. For instance, on the left-hand page of a book, the left white margin should be a little bit wider than the right white margin—and vice versa on the right-hand page. And always— the bottom margin should be a little bit deeper than the width of the side margin, and also deeper than the top margin.

CHAPTER XI

Visualizing the Advertising Message

The first function of an advertisement is to be "seen"—to secure the attention of the reader. The "ad" must win the reader's eye, either through merit of display or through some other interest-catching quality. Here enters the illustration—the strongest single factor in all advertising; for the illustration is both word and picture, at one and the same time. Illustration can describe as no language can, and it transmits its message at a glance rather than through tedious perusal; for, illustration has merely to be seen; it does not have to be read.

Usually the picture serves to describe the article which the "ad" presents. But a good illustration can very profitably describe the selling point as well as the article. When employed to explain in one quick eye-flash the gist of your message, the picture is likely to usurp a part of the function of a caption—sometimes to take the place of a caption.

For instance, call to mind the picture of a good-looking man wearing a Hart, Schaffner, and Marx suit. It speaks for itself as strongly as if it were a head-line saying: "H S & M suits have style." Thus one illustration can suggest qualities of a product more vividly than any number of words, nor can mere words create as vivid and convincing an impression. Unillustrated words often fail even to win a superficial reading, while a picture seldom fails to draw a glance.

To tell a story with pictures you may find that the pen-and-ink style, just the plain "line" cut, works best. Most newspaper cartoons are of this style. Even when the smoothness of printing-stock surface permits the use of a photographic half-tone, the pen-and-ink illustration is likely to be preferable, for it has a dash and a vim, a natural strength and a rugged action which the half-tone often lacks.

The ideal illustration performs two functions—it illustrates the article and also suggests the reasons why the reader should buy. This double purpose in an illustration is the modern style. For instance, one picture shows a happy-faced woman at work with a vacuum sweeper, another portrays an enviable plutocrat at the wheel of a high-powered automobile. In both these cases the half-tone style of illustration is preferable, if feasible, because here your first task is to picture your vacuum cleaner or your machine, while, incidentally, the illustration itself also suggests: "That woman looks contented even when she's sweeping—it must be easy with that vacuum cleaner," or "My, I wish I had a car like that!"

Although illustration can be made so effective as an adjunct to advertising, many advertisers waste pictures. False economy leads them to use any illustration which happens to be on hand. They use it in an "ad" which the illustration does not illustrate. In order to save a few dollars—the few dollars that the new engraving and art work would cost—such pound-foolish persons practically throw away the space for which they have paid hundreds of dollars.

There is a worse offense than this misuse of illustrations which do not illustrate: some pictures not only do not help out, but actually produce a repellent atmosphere about the goods. Take the example of the snake employed to illustrate a food label. This kind of misuse is almost suicidal.

Another danger is the temptation to rely too much upon overused arrows for illustration. Avoid them. Keep in mind the old story about the lad who cried "Wolf!" The cry became an old story; to hear it became a habit. The warning attracted less and less attention the more it was given. So it is with arrows. At first this form of illustration was tremendously attractive, but, so many arrows have been used in so many different ways, that to-day the arrow glides off the reader's eye quite as water does from a duck's back. Yet the arrow still has some value as an aid to other illustrations. You can put action into your "ad" by the use of an arrow. To the reader's eye the arrow seems to fly. It means movement—and for that reason the arrow helps to carry along the reader's eye. You can therefore use arrows to point the way for the reading eye, but you may misuse them so that they clog and block.

The American eye runs from left to right. The Chinese eye does not. The Chinaman reads from bottom to top, whereas the native Hebrew reads his Yiddish from right to left; but the American eye, or the European eye, travels from left to right. So it is that if your arrow does not run from left to right it hinders rather than helps. For instance, paint a black line of type matter across a big outdoor bulletin-board. Over the top of this line, and parallel to it, paint a huge arrow, just as big as the reading line, running from right to left. Beneath this reading line paint another big arrow running from right to left. The words between these two arrows run opposite to the direction of the arrows. They are, therefore, far harder to read than if the arrows were not there—or if the arrows ran from left to right in the same direction as the human eye runs when reading.

In a general way this left-to-right rule holds good in almost any illustration. Suppose that you must picture an automobile. You can do this just as well by having the front at the right and the rear at the left—pointing in the same direction as the eye is accustomed to run; and yet the first fourteen pictures of motor cars which a group of ad men recently investigated, all pointed from right to left—that is, opposite to the natural direction of the reading eye. To emphasize a radiator, it might be best to show the machine facing toward the reader's left. If the illustration be that of a human face, it is better to make the profile point toward the right, rather than toward the left, unless you want to centre special interest on the profile, in which case the face can well be turned toward the left. But, other things being equal, the direction of your illustration should follow the natural course of the human eye—from left to right.

The chief function of illustration is visualization—putting the message in visible form. This part of the task is so big that the mere violation of technical details does not matter much if the design in general strongly visualizes the mes-

About the recent "ad" above, one of the H. S. & M. executives says: "We think this advertisement is best. The illustration tells a good part of the story of good clothing. Combined with this are enough words to deliver our entire message."

sage. Visualization depends on ideas. The idea—or the theme of the illustration—is the first thing that must be conceived. A fair piece of art work, based on the right kind of persuasive idea, may be infinitely better from a standpoint of results than the finest art work based on a mediocre idea.

The idea comes first, and the man who has the ability to create such ideas for effective visualization has the most profitable ability in the field of advertising. From his rough sketch, which simply carries the germ of the idea, the final art work must be developed.

With this rough sketch there must go certain directions, based on certain decisions as to what kind of art work is wanted. For instance, if a boy or girl is to be shown, what kind of a boy or girl? A child of the gutter or a child of the limousine, or a typical American youth? Is the message to be one of the dignity of table silver, or is it to be the slap-you-on-the-back, hail-fellow-well-met slang of the pipe tobacco?

No matter what it is, there should be in the illustration itself a certain appeal—that elusive quality which makes a short story entertaining. This appeal may be in the beauty of a woman's face, or in the joy of a lad who is about to dive into the favorite swimming-hole. Or it may be the aged mother and father sitting together under the evening lamp. Romance is probably the strongest of all these many kinds of appeal. If the illustration can carry with it the romantic quality of a good short story it will have powerful appeal.

Novelty, too, is a quality to be sought when creating illustrations. A novel and original picture will often do wonders. "English Ovals" introduced themselves to the public by a trick picture—the profile of an English type of man, his monocle formed by the large initial "O" of the word Ovals. Then again, in the case of "Meet the Duke of York," another brand of cigarettes was featured by a smoker's hand, holding a lighted cigarette, so arranged that it threw a black silhouette of the duke himself. The refreshing technique of the "Lux" illustrations had much to do with the degree of Lux's success. The "Jonteel" line was built on the eccentric feat-

PEN　　　　　　PENCIL

WASH　　　　　　OIL

The question of what kind of drawing or painting to use, depends on two things: (1) The Subject; (2) The Medium. The usual newspaper advertisement should be in pen-and-ink, because the paper itself is so rough that fine-screen half-tones are impossible. Good magazines can accommodate any style of illustration. If the subject requires photographic treatment, the wash-drawing is best. If the subject requires brutal poster-like technique, the pen-and-ink is best—providing the picture is for use in a publication. (Above drawings used by courtesy of the Strathmore Paper Company.)

ures of an unheard-of bird. "The Bluebird for Happiness" introduced a washing-machine by the novelty of a symbol.

There are many ways of illustrating an idea. The cheapest and the easiest method is by way of the photograph. There are three different kinds of photographs:

1. The straight photograph, with fairly sharp detail.
2. The retouched photograph, with some detail eliminated and other detail emphasized by art work laid over the photograph.
3. The soft-focus photograph, where the detail is blurred and where the general effect is the impressionistic quality of a wash-drawing.

The wash-drawing is like the photograph in that it carries all tones of gray from black to white, although it is done entirely with a brush.

Art work in pencil and in crayon is desirable for certain styles of illustration. Crayon is usually heavy and best used for poster work, whereas pencil is light and dainty, and may be used for illustration either on fine paper, such as magazine stock, or on coarse paper, such as newspaper stock.

There are several ways of making a line-drawing, by using either pen-and-ink, crayon, or dry brush. With pen-and-ink you can obtain a great range of results, from the finely modelled realistic effect to the very flat decorative effect. Although a crayon drawing is made with a crayon, a line cut can be made from it. This is very effective in achieving certain qualities that you cannot get either with a pen or brush. Dry-brush drawings have a distinctive quality all their own. An artist makes these by first dipping his brush in ink and then wiping it off on a blotter, so that there is little ink left on the brush when it is applied to the paper.

The Ben Day—which is a tinted surface laid on during the course of plate-engraving—makes possible all kinds of combinations with all kinds of line-drawings, to the result of a highly artistic technique. Ben Day screens can either be laid on a white surface, making dots or lines on white paper, or

VISUALIZING THE ADVERTISING MESSAGE 93

white dots or lines can be etched into large black surfaces, making them gray instead of solid black. This latter method often gives very pleasing results. It is a rule with some magazines to Ben Day every large mass of black, so that their pages will not be too jumpy in appearance.

Illustrations in colors, there are several varieties:

1. Water-color drawings.
2. Pastels.
3. Oil-paintings.

Although the oil-painting has been used considerably, the tendency in advertising has been toward the water-colors, in pastel treatment—that is, with delicate flat tints of dainty color. This forms a fetching illustration and yet one which does not call too much attention to itself. Modesty is a quality of a good illustration; for the art work in an advertisement is only to help achieve the general result. The art work should be designed to strengthen the advertising message. The advertisement should not be designed to show off the art work.

The kind of drawing or illustration you should use depends on several different factors—the main one being that of medium. First, the mechanical requirements determine a great part of the decision as to what style to adopt. For instance, the newspaper, with its soft, rough printing stock and its high-speed presses, demands either open pen-and-ink, or some similar technique. The magazines, on the other hand, use highly coated stock, which permits the use of almost any kind of art work. The kind of audience to which the advertisement must appeal also helps a great deal to determine the quality of the illustration. Even the editorial quality of the publication in which the advertisement is to appear should have an influence as to the kind of illustration that is to be used.

But, of course, the dominant factor in selecting the method of visualization is the selling message itself. No illustration is worth the space that it takes unless it does more than its proportionate share toward carrying that selling message into the reader's heart and mind.

The size of the advertisement will also have a bearing on the style of illustration. The question, too, of cost will enter. If you can afford only $5.00 for illustration, then you had better stick to photographs. If you have $50 to spend, then you can get a pen-and-ink drawing. If you want a good wash-drawing, you will probably have to pay upward of $100. A fine painting in colors, by one of the best artists, will cost from $250 to $1,000 per illustration.

Not many years ago there were two kinds of art—true art and commercial art. But to-day many of the best artists are commercial artists. This is not wholly due to the fact that these leaders in art can get large fees for doing commercial art work. Rather it is because advertising has so improved that its art work is now on a high plane.

CHAPTER XII

Preliminary Analysis by the Retail Advertiser

With a working knowledge of the principles and mechanics of advertising, the problem begins to become specific. How you should advertise, depends upon whether your business is retail and local—or wholesale and national. Even if it is the latter, you must nevertheless know something of the retail. The local problem is fundamental to any advertising plan. For a nation is only a collection of towns and counties.

There are about one million retail stores in the United States. Many of them are general, but hundreds of thousands of them are special. Many are the result of accident. Others have been planned—even to the extent of their being part of a chain of several thousand stores, as, for example, the five- and ten-cent store syndicates and the A & P groceries.

Usually a store's "product"—that is, its merchandise—is the result of the kind of patronage which the store enjoys. The dealer keeps what his trade wants, and what his trade wants often depends upon the location. This factor, in turn, determines what kind of people come into his store.

There are half a million "neighborhood" stores—little grocery stores and corner candy stores. They are the outcome of the public's desire for convenience. Their best advertising is possibly the handbill which boys distribute through the neighborhood on Friday to announce special "bargains" for Saturday. Such advertising, plus a clean store, attractive windows, and courteous treatment, are the first trade attracters for such merchants. But, if such a dealer desires to expand his business into a city-wide store, or to duplicate his store by the establishment of others here and there throughout the city, then he must use advertising more thoroughly. He must find out what his "product" is—that is, what his goods are, and to whom they will appeal. This investigation will determine where he shall locate his stores, and, also, what kind of a merchandising policy he shall follow.

Instead of an aggressive phase of a store's business, advertising may be a necessary defense. This is particularly true of the smaller communities, where more and more the mail-order houses are fighting for a foothold and wielding their wonderful weapons of publicity. When these distant mercantile institutions do get the trade, it is because they know how to advertise. It is their presentation of picture and price which starts the orders through the mails to such an extent that the letters received by some mail-order houses keep many motor-trucks busy every day—just to carry the orders from the post-office to the office-building.

But before you advertise, analyze. Analysis is the best way to find out anything. First, analyze the kind of store you have. Is it high-grade? Does it make its appeal through quality? Or is it popular because you can make low prices? If it is of the exclusive type, you can count but a small part of the population as possible prospects. If your trade is built on good values and occasional or frequent bargains (which are extra good values), then the majority of the rank and file are potential customers. In such a case, the bigger your business the greater your gains, for even though you make but little on each sale, you can depend upon volume of business for your profit.

To determine what class of trade to go after you should know the statistics of your community. You should know that in the ordinary town of half a million, over one-third of the population have an income of less than $50 a week per family. So, if you go after that less than $50-per-week kind of trade, you may have many customers. But, your sales will mostly be of the necessities of life. You must talk to such people plainly. You cannot whisper to them in graceful similes. You must speak out in plain English. To induce them to enter your store, you cannot rely on a subtle style. Your argument must tingle with economy, durability, and dollar-and-cent quality.

Top "ad" is of 1920—lower one of 1906. The latter was crude but possessed good selling value. Picture and price are also featured in the "Find-Yourself-in-this-Picture" advertisement. Carl R. Hoffmann, Ingersoll advertising manager, says: "This is the best merchandising 'ad' of the year. We have found that people are curious enough to find themselves in the picture or in the list, whichever the case happens to be, and then to study the watches that are designated for their use. We always feel that we can depend on an advertisement of this kind when we really need business."

When you know who your possible customers are, and what you have to offer them, your next analysis will lead you to the question of how to bring the people to your goods. You must find out how to rouse a desire for your goods in your prospects in the quickest and most economical way.

Of all the possible natural virtues in a retailer's advertising, that of timeliness is perhaps the greatest aid to success. Timeliness can be created. For instance, if a store in a neighboring city has burned down, you can arrange for a sale of the remaining goods, and in that way capitalize the element of timeliness. This kind of strategy may be somewhat artificial, but in sales of bought-up bankrupt stocks, this application of the timeliness appeal often has a sound basis on the fact that in this way exceptional merchandise-values are really made possible.

But no healthy, substantial, permanent business success can be built up with the bankrupt or fire-sale idea as its backbone. The main appeal of most goods is simply that they are less in price—either less than they were, or less than the usual prices in other stores.

The right appeal may make a success of an advertising campaign which otherwise would fail. An example of this is the experience of a certain piano store in a Western town. Business was dull. The proprietor tried slashes in prizes, contests, and all that sort of thing, apparently without success. Finally, he hit upon a new idea. He created this theme for his advertising: "Keep the young folks at home." This set the mothers and the fathers in the vicinity to thinking. Here was a vital reason why they should buy a piano. Business came fast as a result.

"How much shall I spend?" is another problem that confronts the retail advertiser. A big department store can afford to spend from 2 to 3% of its gross income. A store just beginning generally has to spend a higher percentage of its gross income than does the store already established. One of New York's greatest department stores spent 5% of its gross income for years, until it got a firm foothold; but now the name of that store is known to everybody, and its present advertising expenditure is only about 3%.

PRELIMINARY ANALYSIS BY RETAIL ADVERTISER 99

Some department stores have to continue to spend much more than others to get business. For instance, in a certain coast city the owners of one big institution found that their advertising averaged a return of about $100 worth of business for every inch of newspaper space they used, whereas another similar institution in the same city secured only $60 worth of business for each inch of space. Experience is the guide to the knowledge of how much to spend. Your solution depends largely on what kind of a store you have. In a specialty store, for instance, it is not too much to appropriate 5% for advertising, based on the total volume of sales. If your store does $100,000 worth of business a year in a specialty line, you can well afford to pay $5,000 a year for advertising. And if you do $500,000 worth of business you can afford to pay $25,000 a year for advertising. This principle covers all specialty stores in furniture and in women's apparel. Also it holds true in regard to installment houses.

But when you come to groceries the advertising could not be 5%. The margin is so small that 5% expense in advertising would probably cause the year to show a loss rather than a profit. Even the big grocery retailer who seeks to reach the public through newspaper advertising must keep his advertising appropriation down around 2 or 2½%; if he does $100,000 worth of business, his advertising would probably cost $2,000 or $2,500.

This principle may vary even with grocery stores if they have other departments in connection with them which will yield sufficient profit to warrant an additional advertising expense. A store which deals in drugs in addition to groceries may be able to spend 3 to 4% on advertising, while a big store selling only groceries will not. The reason is that the profit on drugs is great enough to absorb some of the expense involved in the extra advertising of the store which carries that long-margin merchandise in addition to groceries.

The healthiest sign in connection with any retail store is an increase in business and a decrease in advertising expense. The proportionate advertising expense may decrease as the volume of business increases if the advertising has both selling-value and also that subtler value of confidence creation which builds up a clientèle. This is illustrated by the fact that in one city a department store was doing $3,000,000 worth of business on an expenditure of 2½%. The "copy" was written by a certain advertising manager who changed his position. He went down the street to another department store, which was spending 4% of its gross revenue on advertising. But this latter department store continued to spend 4%, even though the advertising was now directed by the same man who had been able to get the business for the other store on an expenditure of 2½%. The reason was that the public had more faith in the announcements of the former store. Therefore, each inch of space pulled more trade than did that of the other store; and so, though one used more advertising than the other, the expense on a percentage basis was only 2½% in the first case and 4% in the other.

If yours is an exclusive specialty store, basing its appeal on style, yet doing business in the same way as a big department store, then your best advertising may be to establish yourself next to a big department store, so as to make the smartness of your window display divert trade your way. But you may also need a fairly large "ad" now and then to suggest the superior style and the low prices which your specialization is supposed to accomplish. If your specialty store's appeal is wider—if, for instance, you do a credit clothing business—then a greater volume is possible. If such a store has a possible popular appeal, you can afford to advertise much more extensively than the other of more limited possible patronage.

The classified columns of the newspapers are sometimes a profitable means of publicity. For instance, a little store on a side street may advertise quite effectively by using the "Want Ad" columns. As no merchant can afford to spend more than a certain proportion of the amount of business that it is possible to get, it would be wasteful for the usual small side-street merchant to try to use large "ads" in the ordinary display columns of a big newspaper. He can probably get as much business as he can take care of if he uses the "Want Ads" judiciously.

The average retail advertiser has to pay to-morrow's expenses out of to-day's receipts. Retail advertising must be of the action-producing kind. Of course it aims to create a flavor—to build an institutional atmosphere in favor of the store. But above all, it seeks to make to-day's advertising pay for itself in to-morrow's sales.

To sell is the main aim of retail advertising. But this selling must be accomplished in a careful way. Your store may increase its business materially for a time if you use exaggeration in your "ads." But, exaggeration does not pay in the long run. It does not build good-will. It does not bring customers back to you again—which, after all, is the real purpose of attracting people to your store. You can't exaggerate for more than a few days, or for a few weeks. For, at the end of that time, you will probably either have to change your store's name, or move.

Meanwhile, the first dollars spent on such advertisements may seem to pull good response; but gradually people discover your deceit, and, as time goes on, instead of a dollar's worth of advertising attracting $50 worth of business, it will bring diminishing returns, and sooner or later will mean failure for any retail merchant. The retail store depends for its success on the cumulative result that comes from the fact that the customer of to-day gets some one else as an additional customer for to-morrow. So—although your primary aim is to sell—you must always temper your copy with the understanding that your final success must be built on the favorable atmosphere that comes from honest advertising.

Part of the value of your advertising will consist in the cumulative good-will publicity which will incidentally result from the selling effectiveness of your copy. Your advertising must not only carry your message to the old friends of your store, it must make them more friendly, and it must also make new friends for you if your business is to grow.

CHAPTER XIII

Analysis of Retail Appeal

If you use many pages in boastful description of the quality of your merchandise you will not get as much direct result as with less space devoted to a straight description of values. Why should people come into your store to-morrow if they simply know your goods are good? They can come in the next day just as well. But if you advertise a bargain —well, that's different. That particular lot of goods may all be sold out by to-morrow afternoon. Therefore, the public decides it is better to come in to-morrow morning. This fact of human nature makes price the dominant feature in retail advertising.

Now and then you find exceptions from this general principle that retail advertising must be done through price emphasis. If yours is a "class" store, such as an exclusive furniture store, you may ignore price. In this case, your business will be comparatively small. You can grow gradually without the use of the price appeal. But a store which seeks a universal business, which tries to win trade in the east, north, south, and west side of the community, can hardly get along without the price appeal.

One big store recently tried to prove that this principle was wrong. They sought to establish a theory that people do not want prices and that they seek simply the knowledge that the goods can be had at a fair price. So this concern discontinued newspaper advertising and put its messages on outdoor, painted bulletin-boards. One sign announced that kitchen utensils could be bought at this store. Another specialized on cut glass, etc. These announcements simply told the people what could be had at that store at "reasonable prices." This method was supposed to bring as much trade

ANALYSIS OF RETAIL APPEAL 103

to the store as if prices were emphasized. But the experimenter had to go back into the newspapers. Now he is trying to make his newspaper copy carry that same kind of message. But such a message has little appeal; it does not persuade—it simply advises. It merely says in effect: "We are doing business, and we are handling merchandise and we won't overcharge you."

Price, nine times out of ten, is the appeal that wins. But price in itself does not insure success. There has to be real service along with price. Service is of vital importance even when price competition is keen. Service means good quality, general courtesy, and helpfulness, the ability to handle a person's business a little better, a little more satisfactorily than the other fellow. In fact, certain stores can sell on service entirely, stores such as high-class florists, or high-grade jewellers; but most stores must win their patrons on the ground that customers cannot only get good service but also save money if they buy from that particular store.

In the matter of "copy" the necessity for price emphasis may carry the advertiser into a danger—he is apt to make his "ad" a veritable price-list. In some cases you may simply record cut prices and win out; but as a rule the advertiser who keeps away from the catalogue style and puts into his price argument a further appeal, based on quality or utility, is likely to succeed better than the man who simply lists his prices.

Between the kind of retail advertising which merely lists a lot of prices and the style which devotes itself exclusively to a single article there is a golden mean. This is the advertising which comprises many items, yet gives each item a concentration, just as if it were a unit "ad" in itself. All these units are harmonized under one theme, and the entire "ad" is a harmonious whole. Many good examples of this are found in the advertising of big department stores. This kind of "copy" unifies the message. It tells one thing at a time. One "ad" may cover fifty different things, but each item is made a separate "rifle-shot." Each is blocked off in an effective way. This makes it easy for the eye to scan the "ad" and find something of especial interest. And when the eye does stop at something that appeals, the reader receives more than just the price. She is subjected to persuasion which tends to create desire—to make her want to buy whether she had expected to or not.

"Specialty" stores—such as those which specialize in haberdashery or men's apparel, or in women's apparel, or in high-class furniture—have found that the best kind of an advertisement is the kind that talks about one thing and covers it fully. For the main appeals of stores like these must be service, or style, or exclusiveness rather than price. Such a store, therefore, usually concentrates the entire "ad" on one specific thing.

For instance, in advertising fine furniture, this is what one successful specialty merchant does: He shows a picture of a chair and describes its exquisite beauty and fine workmanship; he phrases and pictures the product in the most alluring way, without mention of price. The price of so exquisite a chair is probably secondary in the eyes of those exclusive few to whom this class of goods will appeal. Such people are more impressed by suggestion of style or prestige, or artistic origin, than by mere dollar-saving. In this sort of exclusive specialty-store advertising, unification of copy may be best—even to the extent of making one "ad" speak only of one article. Here the task is to create desire to such a degree that price can be entirely ignored.

There are many other retail advertisers besides the departmental institutions and the specialty stores. Automobile agencies come under the retail class, although, really, their advertising is simply localized national advertising. Insurance offices come under the retail advertising class. Dairy companies, public-utility corporations, and other organizations of that kind are also in this category. But with most of these there is no problem as to whether to include many, few, or only one item in their advertising "copy." The object of their advertising is usually a single thing on which they can concentrate with an appeal filled with persuasive suggestion.

The small retailer has to get more business with propor-

The recent advertisement at right, as well as the twenty-year-old one below, shows the kind of illustration that demonstrates what the product is and how it works. The use of children in the modern picture is a step forward.

In referring to the "ad" at the right, R. G. Burns, advertising manager of the Macey Company, says: "We consider this the best advertisement we have ever produced, because one of the greatest selling arguments for a Sectional Bookcase is the fact that the initial installation can be small and added to as the family needs more room for their books. We think that the caption 'Expanding Minds need Expanding Bookcases' very well expresses everything there is to be said about our Sectional Bookcases."

tionately less advertising expense. To do this his copy must breed confidence and create a permanent clientèle. If he fails to build up a patronage of people who automatically come to his store for their needs (whether they come as a result of an advertised bargain or not) then his volume of business is apt to be entirely dependent on his advertising. His business then will be proportionately smaller than if he also possessed a cumulative patronage.

This is the usual misfortune of the store that exaggerates. There are many tragic examples of stores which used to lead, but which are now second-raters—and for no other reason than that their advertising was insincere. Most states now have laws which make it a misdemeanor to employ fraudulent advertising. Several stores have been prosecuted for statements that certain goods were worth more than they really were. One big store was prosecuted and its manager was arrested because he advertised a piano for $125 which he said was worth $250. Experts proved in court that the piano was not worth $250. But the legal dangers of exaggeration in advertising are not as great as the terrible peril that ten years from now a business may go to smash simply because a merchant allows exaggeration in his advertising to-day.

The undermining process of exaggeration is subtle. It becomes visible slowly. Public suspicion gradually results from untruthful "copy." This takes patronage away from the store. The merchant may go on for a long time and seem to get more business. But the biggest community is so small that eventually this kind of policy proves suicidal. People compare notes and gradually the tide turns against the store.

But most merchants nowadays keep clear of old-time circus methods of exaggeration. They know too well this rigid principle of advertising. They know that if they stoop to deceptive advertising their copy will pull less and less as the years go on, and instead of building the business, will tend to undermine it.

Although most retail advertisers take their advertising seriously, and realize how much it costs, and appreciate that it is the only way to increase their business, the average retailer pays too little attention to his advertising. The reason lies, as usual, in human nature. It is easier to buy than to sell. Any one would rather sit in an office and have a salesman try to get him to buy something than to sit down and work out some scheme with ink and paper by which to make people feel that they ought to come and buy something from him.

The usual retailer is therefore likely to be just a "buyer." Of course he has to buy his merchandise wisely, so as to give proper value; but if he paid as keen attention to the sales development of his business—to the advertising of his business—he would progress with greater strides. No matter what values you have to offer, if people don't know about them they are well-nigh worthless; no matter how desirable your goods may be, if you don't create a desire in their favor you fall short.

Newspapers find that specialty-store merchants, who spend several thousands a year in advertising, frequently try to write their "ads" in five minutes, "while the boy waits." Some of them hand in an "ad" to occupy a large space, and yet they sketch it on the back of a calling card.

There are some retailers who so clearly visualize the purpose of their advertising that they have their advertisements set up by their own printers. In this way a store can radiate an atmosphere of artistic distinction. Many a wise advertiser spends an extra $10 or so every time he prepares an "ad," simply in order to get the prettiest border, the most attractive kind of type, and the daintiest possible taste into his store announcements. He has his own printer compose the type and turn the completed form over to the newspaper —despite the fact that he could get the newspaper to set up the "ad" gratis if he were content with ordinary typography.

Another very important detail in advertising is that of "position." Specialty stores, as a rule, appeal to either men or women, or to some definite class. Such advertisers have to choose where, in a particular newspaper, their "ad" will do the most good. A haberdasher, for instance, may want to be on the sporting page. A department store may put one little "ad" opposite the women's or the society page, and then place their large "ad" wherever they can. The little "ad" calls attention to their main announcement on another page. Some big stores believe in this method so thoroughly that they have their general "ad" on the back page of the newspaper and their particular items, referring to women's garments and so on, on the women's page, and their "ads" of men's garments on the men's page.

When it comes to "Want Ads," attention to position may pay. You should be careful to select the proper classification. And even the small merchant in the country unconsciously pays close attention to position. You will see in almost any weekly paper of towns of less than 10,000, little items in regard to bargains at the local store interspersed among the local news paragraphs. Sometimes these are put in among the personals, and sometimes among bits of local news. Such advertising frequently costs more than the usual rate. In the usual small paper, where the regular inch rate may be 15 cents or 10 cents, the rate for these local items may figure up to 30 cents or 60 cents per inch. Preferred position is the reason why the local advertiser uses those expensive little local lines instead of regular display space.

CHAPTER XIV

Methods of Retail Advertising

Newspaper advertising is not the only kind that the retailer may profitably use. The circular letter is often effective, although it is hard to make this kind of "direct" advertising yield an adequate profit, because, as compared with the newspaper, it costs so much to print and mail. The newspaper will reach over 5,000 people at approximately less than a cent per line. The circular cannot reach 1,000 people for under $25.

Here again it depends on the kind of merchandise which you have to advertise. If yours is a high-priced specialty with a strong appeal to a certain class, you may be able to construct a selected mailing list. In such a case, the goods sold may yield you so wide a margin of profit that the circular will more than pay for itself; at least waste circulation will be practically eliminated. But for a business which seeks customers from all classes of people, and which works on a limited margin of profit, it is difficult to use the expensive circular for general attraction of trade.

The biggest merchants use "direct" advertising—but always as a secondary method—merely to reinforce the newspaper advertising. A large department store may have a mailing list of 50,000. With electric addressing-machines and mechanical folding devices it is possible to put out circulars to all these customers. Even such stores very seldom attempt this mailing, except as a supplement to newspaper advertising and in connection with a few special sales. When a store has a long list of charge customers to whom monthly statements must be sent, any circulars may be enclosed in the envelopes with the bills. Such direct mail work is likely to pay for itself because there is no expense for postage.

110. A SHORT COURSE IN ADVERTISING

Many retailers advertise with novelties, specialties, and souvenirs. These are not supposed to sell anything. They seldom result in direct returns which will pay for their expense. They are simply meant as builders of good-will toward the merchant who pays for them. Their cost per person reached is greater by far than the most expensive newspaper or the most elaborate piece of mail matter.

There is no question but that there is only one sure medium for the retail advertiser who is big enough to serve a community-wide trade—and that medium is the newspaper. If the advertiser is so localized that he can only serve people around his particular neighborhood, then the circular distributed by the boy after school may be best. But if he is, or can become, of sufficient size to make a bid for business almost anywhere in his community, then the newspaper is the medium, first, last, and always. One reason for this is that the newspaper enjoys a home interest. It has a personal appeal—it deals with local affairs of intimate interest to every reader. It tells of the actions of the city government, to which the reader pays taxes, or records the demolition of a building which the reader has frequently seen. It has an ever-fresh appeal. It quickens the reader's interest every day, if it be a daily—or every week, if it be a weekly. It always offers something new.

A painted sign may seek to advertise a certain kind of shoe. You may pass this sign every day, yet you will really see it about once every three months; and possibly you may not consciously see it even then. The sign has no fresh appeal. You may know that it is there, but after your first attentive glance it fails to open your mind enough further to stimulate it. It possesses nothing new enough, or personal enough, to attract your repeated attention.

A good newspaper is a sort of institution. Men will almost fight for their favorite newspapers. A paper may gain as strong a hold upon a man, almost, as his church. The majority of people owe nearly all they know to their newspaper. In a political campaign a newspaper often shows its potential power. What the paper says carries weight—that is, if

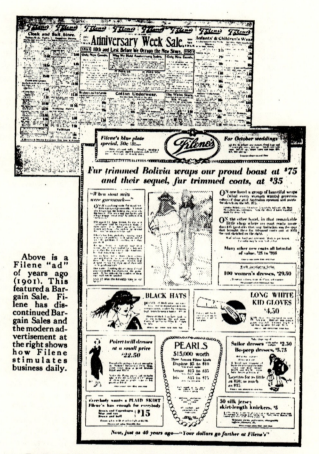

Above is a Filene "ad" of years ago (1901). This featured a Bargain Sale. Filene has discontinued Bargain Sales and the modern advertisement at the right shows how Filene stimulates business daily.

Typographically the announcement at top featuring Filene's Tenth Anniversary Week is rather uninviting compared to the recent announcement below, which is open, easy to read, comprehensive, and forceful.

it is an honest newspaper. If it is not honest people do not believe in it. No matter how clever or verbally forceful its assertions may be, such a paper will not carry weight, even though its circulation may be as big as that of any paper in town.

A real paper with a time-tried clientèle has, therefore, the power to carry any message; that is why it can carry advertising messages to the profit of the advertiser. These facts make the question of newspaper rates a hard puzzle. No one can arbitrarily say, for instance, that each thousand of circulation is worth a quarter of a cent per line, because it is not worth that in some papers, and in others it may be worth more; for some papers are almost Bibles in the homes into which they go.

A puzzling question in retail advertising is whether to use the morning or the afternoon papers? The answer depends on the papers. One morning paper may actually go into more homes than any evening paper in the community. It may reach more women. And yet, for advertising things which appeal to women, it is usually argued that the evening paper is the one to use. The evening paper holds that the housewife does not have time during the day to look at the morning paper, whereas she reads the evening paper in her leisure hours. But here, too, any effort at a definite law is worthless. The soundest principle is simply that the best paper is the one which will reach the greatest number of prospects in the strongest way at the lowest cost.

There are many store conditions which tend to determine a retailer's advertising methods. For instance, whether your "ads" should appear on Monday, or Wednesday, or Friday, or when, is a question which depends on the kind of store—and an analysis of your individual problem. If you are advertising bargains in competition with all the other stores in town, you will probably want your advertising to appear the day previous to the one which is most commonly regarded as "Bargain Day" in your town. In some cities, by common consent, Friday is "Bargain Day." Consequently, Thursday is a good time to advertise, if you offer bargains in general competition. The shopping public will be down-town on Friday, and it is easier to get them to walk from some other store to yours than it is to persuade them to take the trouble to come all the way down-town just to look over the merchandise you advertise.

Some advertisers may better choose other days than Thursday and Friday. If your "ad" is in a paper containing a thousand "ads," it is less effective than if it were in one containing a hundred. If, therefore, you need not depend upon the Friday shopping crowd, perhaps you had better use the Saturday or Monday editions, when the paper will have fewer "ads" against which yours must compete. There is no rule as to this point, either. It depends entirely on the particular store. In fact, many stores find it profitable to go into the papers on Sunday. The theory is that despite the vast amount of advertising on that day, people have more time on Sunday to study over the advertisements.

But there is one little point in connection with retail newspaper advertising to which the wise retailer is giving attention, more and more every day. That is the co-operation on the part of the sales people in the store. Formerly, the usual advertiser would simply trust that the people in the store would see the store's advertising in the papers. Now he makes his staff look at the announcements. Store efficiency demands that sales people keep up with the store's advertising. Copies of each day's "ads" are usually posted around every good store. In some stores the management actually holds classes to explain the things offered, so that every employee will be intelligent when a customer comes in as the result of the advertising.

In the last analysis the sales person is the biggest factor in advertising. The vice-president of a nationally-known glove industry recently stated that in seven cases out of ten the sales person determines what brand of glove a woman shall buy. Most people think that actual public demand is all-powerful. But in reality the demand is largely in the sales person's mind. To illustrate that fact a manufacturer told this story about a store in Detroit: The manager of the glove department said to him: "We can't sell your brand—the demand is for such-and-such a glove." The manufacturer asked him how he knew. "Why," replied the buyer, "nine people out of ten who come in here for gloves ask for your competitor's brand."

The manufacturer challenged the truth of the buyer's conclusion. To test it out they stood by the glove counter and watched. Of seven people who came in for gloves not one asked for any particular brand. They all simply asked for "a pair of gloves," and the sales girl said: "You mean such-and-such a glove?" In most cases the customer said "Yes." In this way the "demand" in the mind of the sales girl was interpreted by the department manager as a real demand in the mind of the public. And so the co-operation of the dealer's sales people is about the biggest asset a manufacturer can get in his retail distribution—and, likewise, this same intra-store co-operation is necessary to the dealer if he is to make his advertising approach the ideal of efficiency.

There are a good many advertising aids which the retail advertiser can get at no expense to himself. These are the helps which manufacturers offer. These may be window displays, or even circular letters which the manufacturer will get out and mail to the retailer's customers, in behalf of the retailer. Many manufacturers will supply the retailer with free booklets with the dealer's name imprinted on the back. These advertise the manufacturer's product which the retailer has on sale. Some manufacturers even offer moving signs, costing from $10 to $30 apiece. These are loaned absolutely without charge to the dealer.

The wise dealer can use a good many of these helps. If, with these, he uses some newspaper advertising, he can build up a strong demand in favor of his merchandise. This co-operative advertising makes the store's publicity less expensive and more effective, and means more business for the dealer.

When special window displays, especially personal demonstrations, are arranged, it is sometimes profitable for the dealer to pay half the expense and the manufacturer the other half. This, too, depends upon conditions. If the dealer handles the goods exclusively it is more logical for him to divide the expense than if every rival merchant in town also has them on sale. But the mere loaning of a window to advertise a manufacturer's product costs a dealer money.

Good window space on a popular street makes a retail store rental worth over twice what it should otherwise cost. In other words, a thousand feet of floor space in an obscure street will cost, say $3,000 a year, while that same floor space on a prominent street will cost $10,000 a year. This $7,000 more is the cost of location—partly convenience of location and also because the windows invite the passers-by and thus attract trade into the store.

The average dealer does not realize how expensive his windows are, and so many a window goes undressed. Big department stores do realize. They know that their windows are worth all the attention they can give them. They know that a window is like a newspaper. To use it as an advertising medium costs nothing but a little labor. Even a small dealer can get from manufacturers all sorts of help with which to keep the windows continually fresh and attractive. Frequent change of window is as important as change in newspaper copy.

These same principles apply to counter display, by the arrangement of attractive features and a general and particular presentation of merchandise. In former days necessaries like dress goods, silks, and cottons were put near the front. Nowadays luxuries and semi-luxuries, things that appeal to the vanity, to the eye, are put to the front where people have to pass them before getting to the necessities; for people will go anywhere for necessities—even to the topmost floor of a store.

Retail advertising has produced too many freakish methods. Cleverness is good while the line of cleverness is new, but when it gets old it creates a sorry spectacle. As a result, the clever kinds of advertising—far-fetched contests, such as guessing the number of beans in a jar in a window, and many other stunts of that sort—are rapidly becoming obsolete.

Meanwhile, the value of straightforward publicity, by which you tell people what you have and the reasons why they ought to buy from you, is becoming ever more widely appreciated.

CHAPTER XV

Advertising's Part in Department Stores

The department-store merchant has advertising problems beyond those which confront the usual retailer, because the merchandise he sells covers so wide a range—almost everything from pins to pianos, from garden seeds and tools to diamonds. The machinery of a department store's activities is tremendous. Because of its peculiar organization and its size it has developed an organization peculiar to itself.

A department store should be distinctive. It should become an institution. To some stores people grow so loyal that they swear by them. They would not go to others. They talk of them as if they were part of their lives. They even argue for them as against the favorite store of some one else. Almost every department store, no matter how big, possesses a personality of its own. Perhaps it may depend upon a certain kind of service, or an atmosphere. If it lacks personality—if it is just a huge, lifeless project—then it must depend entirely on low price to be even a mediocre success.

How can a store build up this distinctiveness? That is the greatest question the department store has to face. It can help create this distinctive atmosphere through advertising. One store accompanies its dignified Cheltenham style of typography with dainty illustrations. Another store seems to use naught but square-cornered, black-face Gothic. Yet, many a time a person will go into the former store and ask for something that has been advertised by the latter—and vice versa. It is possible, nevertheless, to build up distinctiveness by means of advertising, but a concomitant with this must be a steady effort to make a store's service and its whole atmosphere individual.

The effort to individualize a department store applies to

the merchandise itself. Some department stores want to be themselves and nothing else. Many department stores even insist that all their stock bear their own trade-mark. One institution in New York, which does a business of $30,000,000, has hardly a nationally advertised trade-mark in the entire store. If they do use the products of nationally advertised industries, they call them by some brand of their own. They refuse to carry nationally advertised goods, even though they lose money thereby. They want their store to be absolutely distinctive. They desire even more than a mere atmosphere of their own; they want all their wares to stand in the store's own name. They will not push any particular manufacturer's line in any way lest they help to build up a demand for his goods in their store; for if they should push a maker's brand, the manufacturer would have the upper hand and could make them buy his goods at his own terms;—that is what they fear.

"We have to stand behind our goods, anyway. If anything goes wrong we have to make good. Why, then, shouldn't we brand them with our own name as long as we are held responsible for what we sell?" That is the way the manager of a big Eastern department store sums up this tendency to bury the manufacturers' trade-marks and push the store's own private brands.

But there is another side to this question worthy of serious consideration for the average, for the majority of stores. Many millions of dollars are spent by national advertisers. Their goods are already half sold by their own advertising. Often no more is necessary than for the local store to say that it sells such and such products—or merely to show them. Many of the new school of merchants are taking advantage of the tremendous national advertising force to which they can very profitably tie their stores.

Although it is true that many big institutions prefer to push goods under their own trade-marks, some stores boast of the number of factory-trade-branded lines that they carry. And there is one exception to any department store's tendency to keep away from nationally advertised goods—that

At left, an advertisement of twenty years ago. Below, a double-spread of recent days. The contrast suggests "from the ridiculous to the sublime."

This advertisement is not as "clever"—it is not so unusual—it probably attracts less attention than the jackass and cupid in the former "ad" shown above. But what good is attention if it be not favorable? What does cleverness gain when it calls attention toward itself and away from the product?

is when it has secured exclusive rights to sell a certain well-known brand.

It is natural that the advertising policy of a department store should largely influence its buying policy. As its managerial organization is largely one of buyers, the very personnel of a big store's machinery is closely related to advertising. As a rule, the active head is the merchandise manager, under whom come the buyers. Each buyer manages a different department. Each buyer is really the sales manager of his department.

The buyer is called a "buyer" because he spends the greatest amount of time in actual buying; yet the purpose of buying is to achieve the greatest possible volume of sales. The better the department manager buys, the more successful he should be as a sales manager; but, many a very good buyer is a poor salesman or sales manager, and more than fortunate is he who possesses in a marked degree both buying ability and selling ability.

Every buyer, each at the head of a different department, is subject to the merchandise manager, who is, indeed, the head buyer. It is usually he, with the advertising manager, who decides the broader questions in regard to advertising. When it comes to a decision in regard to the particular department, the head of that department, the buyer, is called into the conference. Of course a buyer is responsible for the business of his department. If too much money is spent on advertising, his department may show a loss. If the wrong item is advertised, the desired results will be lacking. Therefore, the advertising expense will be too great, the net profit too little. For that reason the buyer has much to say about the advertising.

Thus the departmental manager usually determines what goods shall be advertised. The choice is sometimes based on competition—with the aim of meeting something that has been advertised by some other store. Sometimes the goods are picked for advertisement on account of cut price—for instance, articles that have been bought under price, and so can be sold at less than usual price. Many times, however, the choice is simply based on the seasonableness of the goods. Of the considerations which usually determine what shall be selected for advertisement, timeliness is the greatest factor. For instance, the Christmas season calls forth certain goods to be advertised, regardless of whether they are practically underpriced or not. The summer season calls forth the advertisement of certain other seasonable goods. House-cleaning time occasions the advertisement of cleaning helps, furniture, and so on.

Cut price is sometimes used simply to attract people to the store, so as to get them to buy something in addition to the "leader" advertised. Unfortunately, there is another consideration which often enters into retail advertising—and that is the amount of business done a year ago to-day. The department manager always feels this spur of a previous record. Although conditions may not be ripe for him now to sell the same quantity of goods that he sold a year ago, yet he feels he is falling down if he does not equal or surpass the former figures. This often tempts him to use more advertising than he should, or to cut the price more than he ought.

The department-store organization is managed by an executive head, over the department heads or buyers—the men who direct the sales in each department. Although the buyers have to perform every kind of a duty, and are practically managers of the small stores which comprise the big one, they have little to do with credits of customers; they have nothing to do with the financing of the store; nor do they get up the "ads" in the form in which you see them in the newspapers. The buyer need not know much about the mechanical details of this phase of the work; he may not know one size of type from another, or a half-tone from a zinc etching; yet, really, he is the man who, guided and assisted by the advertising manager, constructs the advertising. And in the department-store business the advertising is all-important.

A department manager must bear advertising in mind every time he considers the purchase of stock for his department; always he must ask himself: "How advertisable is this?" He has to buy on the basis of the goods' appeal to his customers; he knows that he buys simply to sell, and if goods are to sell, they must appeal to the public. He must be able to offer desirable goods at a desirable price, and to do this he must buy with "salability" as the prime consideration.

The advertising manager's office in a department store is, in a way, a clearing-house for the individual advertising ideas of the department heads. The manager's work is highly specialized. Yet it ought to be sufficiently generalized to bring about a harmony among all the different, and often very crude, advertising ideas of all these different buyers. His task is largely to smooth down, polish up, and present the advertising in an attractive and appealing form. The success of the appeals themselves must largely depend on the obvious value of the merchandise offered. Even if an advertising man has little power of diction, or display ability, or other elements of advertising skill, still, if he happens to be in a store where the merchandise is unusually salable, he may win out quite as well as a more brilliant advertisement writer. For department-store advertising is simply *news;* and if the facts are presented pleasantly they will win the business.

There is very little guesswork about department-store advertising. Every cent that is spent on publicity for a buyer is charged up against his department. He knows just how much it costs to "keep the business coming," as far as his particular part of the store is concerned; whether that cost is at a higher percentage than it was a year ago; whether he is getting the same amount of business that he got a year ago; and, with the same amount of advertising, if he is not getting the same amount of business, he knows he has either chosen the wrong goods to advertise or in some other way he has fallen short.

Business conditions, weather, various other elements may make to-day's business different from that of a year ago. These points are given consideration. But still, regardless of all outside factors, the buyer is eternally up against the plain figures of the cost of his advertising as compared with the current volume of his department's business—and here lies the success or failure of a department. The department that does not increase in volume, is regarded as one to be watched by the management; yet, the department that increases in volume and still incurs too great'an advertising expense, is also to be looked after. The big task is to increase the business and to decrease the business-getting expenditures.

Especially when it comes to sales, the departmental buyer selects what stock to feature on the basis of its salability, which means its advertisability. All special goods which are thus to be featured in a sale are chosen by the buyer—often in collaboration with the merchandise or advertising manager, or both. The merchandise manager, who acts as a sort of head buyer, may suggest, and may often initiate, but, as a rule, it is the buyer who says: "That shall go in at 99 cents, and that at 46 cents." He will indicate the prices on those goods—sometimes so low that every such article that he sells will mean a loss to the store, and therefore a red mark against the profit of his department.

He knowingly and willingly marks the goods below cost. He puts in a pair of gloves that cost him $2.05 and marks them $1.95. Every pair he sells means more than 10 cents out of the store's coffers—more, because the overhead and selling cost must also be added to the loss. This simply means that he must sell more goods at regular prices in order to make up for the loss. But, the buyer realizes that this is one way to attract people to his store, so that they may see the service and realize how pleasurable it is to deal there. On the other hand, he may choose seasonable goods for price-slashing, because if these goods are not sold when new, they will have to be sold later at an even greater loss.

Most department stores are built up on advertising. And frequently this advertising is made successful by bargains—made possible by a merchandising ability. For prices, of themselves, will attract trade to a department store. The department store can afford to sell at a loss on some items, because it can sell enough other goods to make up for the losses on the advertised bargains.

Of course all department stores do not make price the keystone of their business-getting. Those few that do not must have some sort of an appeal of class, some exclusive quality of style. Even such stores are apt to resort to the price appeal every now and then. This sort of stimulus is less necessary if there is news value in the advertising—if the copy is of that helpful, instructive, suggestive kind which makes its appeal through timeliness.

Seldom does a buyer initiate a sale in his department of sufficient importance to dominate the entire store, although this is sometimes done by furniture departments. Furniture sales are apt to become the major attraction of a store, for the reason that such merchandise brings in money so fast. A furniture sale may turn over $20,000 or $30,000 a day in a great department store, which means that the store can afford to buy a page, for instance, in the biggest newspapers, and yet have sufficient business to bring the cost of this page advertising down to 2 or 3% of the volume of consequent sales for that one department. But it would be impossible for the notion department, for instance, to hold a sale and try to dominate the store through page advertising. Even if a notion-department buyer got all the business there was in the city in his line on that day, he would not find enough to warrant the cost of big advertising on anything like a 2 or 3% basis.

Sales are usually conducted on an all-embracing sales plan which the advertising manager of the department store conceives and conducts. Some big stores have different sales of this kind almost every week in the year. This week it may be the "Inventory" Sale—next week, the "Opportunity" Sale —another week, the "Anniversary" Sale, and so on, through the "Golden Harvest" Sale, and a lot of other such events. To each of these the different buyers contribute by having their departmental items included in the general event. Many old-established stores hold these sales in almost as conventional and inevitable rotation as the calendar itself. They know now just what kind of a sale they are going to conduct a year hence. They follow through a set schedule of sales events, year in and year out.

CHAPTER XVI

Who and Where Are the Best Prospects?

In almost any selling problem you must analyze the public to find out who and where your best possible prospects are. Conversely, you must look at your product and decide to whom it is impossible to sell. If you have to advertise a luxury, even though it be partly a necessity, you can figure that there are twenty-five million people in the United States who cannot afford it. Possibly you may make them buy, but on the basis of living expenses and income they cannot afford anything but bare necessities. In fact, many authorities hold that of the hundred million people in the United States, there are only five million families who really have sufficient income and enough intelligence to warrant a manufacturer in advertising to them.

Income-tax returns are a great light on the question "Who is able to buy?" Figures, as compiled by the Bankers Trust Company, showed that only 503,050 families had yearly incomes of $4,000 or more—26,000,000 families of less than $4,000 per year. About 85% had incomes of $1,000 or less; 7% had incomes of $1,000 to $2,000; 5¼% incomes of $2,000 to $4,000; and only 2½% had incomes of $4,000 or more. Of course these figures are changing every year.

A few years ago a patented piece of furniture appeared on the market. It was heralded as a wonderful success. Great factories were built to manufacture it. An advertising campaign was opened at an expenditure of $10,000 a month. The inventor thought the resulting royalties would make him rich. One of the most successful advertising managers in New York gave up his position to go into the project on a small salary, with a share of the stock.

The article was put on the market to sell at $20. The average article of its kind usually brought around $7 or $8.

At $20 this specialty had too few possible prospects. A man who was making about $3,000 a year said it was good, but that he could not afford it. The fact that a family with an income of over $3,000 a year couldn't afford this article, helped to explain why the business turned out to be a flat failure.

If the originators had analyzed the statistics to begin with, they would have known that failure was probable because at $20 only about 10% of the people could afford it. Then, too, there would be only about 5% even of those people who would be in the market for such an article. As a result the possible market was limited to less than 1% of the population; and yet they sought to advertise to that handful—using and paying for the space in magazines that reached the whole nation.

Experts have figured out that the usual $3 article will sell five times as easily as a $5 article. This has been proved in connection with specialties which, at first, were sold at prices which seemed exorbitant. In one case, the advertiser cut the price just about in two. Then he tried out the new price in five towns, using the same amount of space in the newspaper as he had used before when his price was twice as much. When he figured up the amount of goods that had been sold in the month under the new price, he found that in those five towns he had sold ten times as much as under the old price. This man's actual net profit was doubled by cutting the price in two. In addition to the fact that reduced prices enable more people to buy, they divert existing business from competitors. That is why lowered prices often mean increased profit, especially in connection with advertised merchandise.

You must not only find out who are able and likely to buy, but you must also find out where they are. You will have to decide whether to try to sell your product to the city trade, or the rural trade, or both. Of course, some articles would be for sale only in the country, and others would have their market only in the city; but there are many things which can be sold in both, and the question then is which market you should develop first.

At left—a magazine page of 1900. Below, the first of a newspaper series of 1920.

This "ad" has these virtues: 1. The layout dominates any newspaper page. 2. It cannot fail to be read by any one who turns to that page. 3. The message itself is the great central thought which classifies Locomobile. All the words in the language could not say more than the two which have been used. 4. The Hare's Motors symbolism of the artist suggests with great power the purposes and ideals of the institution behind the product.

For instance, suppose you are running an insurance company. In every city there are hundreds and hundreds of insurance solicitors—probably every city resident knows two or three people who want to sell him insurance. In the country, on the other hand, there are comparatively few insurance agents. You might think, therefore, that you had better make your insurance company's advertising seek to sell policies by mail in the country; but as a matter of fact there is a greater percentage of available prospects in the towns and cities. One insurance company which tried out the agricultural press found only one rural paper which brought inquiries at as low a cost as the average of the publications which circulated in the cities. This signified that it would cost more to get business from the country than from the city. From then on the company knew where their best field lay.

This question, "Who is my best prospect?" is often decided simply by the nature of the product. For instance, in the automobile field, if a company begins to make a car to sell at a low price, they know that their prospects are those of average means who cannot afford a big car, but who may be able to pay $1,000 for one. Consequently, their appeal must be very different from that of the makers of $5,000 cars. Their methods, their whole system, must be more extensive.

In any consideration of what people comprise your best market, the government census statistics are of great aid. If it weren't for these figures, few would know that almost half the people in the United States live outside of the towns and cities—that the rural population of the United States two years after the war was 50,972,000—over 6,066,000 in villages of less than 2,500 population. And, in the matter of ability to purchase—the average income per family in towns and cities is less than $1,200 per year. In the professional class, lawyers, doctors, etc., the average income is not much over $2,000 per year; but there are 6,000,000 farmers in the United States who average over $2,500 a year net income from their farms.

Statistics also help to answer the question as to whether

At left, a magazine page of 1900. Below, a magazine page of 1920. Both advertise the same instrument—the Pianola.

The old "ad" is all about "us"—"our" product and "our" mission. The new one is about a week-end party—about "you" and "your" good times. More intriguing, isn't it?

to seek to sell to men or to women. Frequently an advertiser may think he is selling to men when really he is selling to women. More men's socks are bought by women than by men, for example; and investigations seem to show that even 55% of all the haberdashery is bought by women. In Wisconsin the State Census Department figures out that the women of that State spend $900,000,000 a year.

Statistics also show where the best markets are when judged from the standpoint of business conditions. You would not advertise in the wheat belt, for instance, if the wheat crop were a failure; nor would you advertise in Aroostook County, Maine, if potato crops were unprofitable. You must make analyses of this kind to avoid advertising waste.

Automobile statistics are a much-used fund of information. Suppose you are selling an automobile accessory: If you know that in one State, a fairly authoritative investigation shows that 24% of the farmers own motors, and that in another State about 29% of them possess motors, and that in a third nearly 50% of them drive cars, then you can well see that the farmer population ought to be reached by your advertising.

Suppose you are advertising one of the many preparations which are designed to straighten out the kinks in the hair of colored people. You may think that there is a very small market for this article, but the fact is that there are nine million colored people in the United States, and if your advertising covers the South a large percentage of the public may be persuaded to buy your product.

Some advertisers use as subjects for illustrating advertisements the familiar figures of the railroad world, the fireman and the engineer. These characters are surrounded with an atmosphere of romance and have an indirect appeal on that ground, but, that aside, such characters, when used in an advertisement, have an extra appeal to all who are interested in the railroad industry, and when you consider that there are two million railroad workers in the United States, you can see what a great audience you are talking to in terms of their daily work.

If the iron and steel industry is badly depressed by indus-

WHO AND WHERE ARE THE BEST PROSPECTS? 131

trial conditions, and production is reduced to a minimum, many who live by their earnings are temporarily unable to buy what you have to sell. This means a large portion of your market is affected, for there are five million who make their living in the iron and steel industry of the United States.

There are probably more farm statistics than any other kind of official statistics, and they frequently help to solve an advertising problem. For example, if you are advertising a stump-puller, where will your best market be? In the North Atlantic States, the farm lands comprise nearly twice as many improved acres as woodland. In the South Atlantic States, the proportion is half and half. Obviously, there is far more stump-pulling to be done in the North than in the South. The knowledge derived from this comparison tells you which is the better market to work.

When the thermos bottle was first put on the market the promoter's idea was that this novelty would be a great accessory to the picnics of the wealthy. As it developed, a tremendous market existed among the factory workers who wanted to take a warm drink to work with them for use at the noon-hour. This discovery gave a wholly different aspect to the marketing problem. Instead of the prospects being a comparative handful of wealthy people, the circle of possible buyers included millions of wage-earners. As a result the entire advertising method underwent a transformation. Increased demand brought increased production, which made it possible to lower the price so as to bring it within reach of the greatest possible number of buyers.

Such has been the history of many a marketing problem. Experience has brought out new facts which have changed the entire plan, and have often resulted in an expansion of the market and a decrease in the price. A knowledge of statistics and an analysis of conditions will often go a great way to save part of the expense which a change of plan always involves.

CHAPTER XVII

Analysis of the Consumer's Attitude

Analyses of prospects to determine how and where to advertise go farther than an inquiry into the ability to buy. They must take in more than the prospects themselves, they must search the conditions which surround those prospects.

These analyses must also cover the conditions of the market. They involve a scrutiny of temporary conditions such as war, permanent conditions such as habits of the trade and, above all, conditions of competition. These factors largely determine what advertising tack to take. Formerly, in advertising a food product the manufacturers never would say that it contained "no alum," but now, when all the pure-food experts are decrying the use of alum in foods, the manufacturers find it advantageous to make their product appear particularly pure by this assertion. These advertisers know that the prospect has formed a prejudice, and talk to the housewife on that basis.

Analyses of conditions also have to do with competition. For instance, a cream-separator concern found that they could not sell at all in Wisconsin and Michigan though they sold very successfully in New England. They analyzed and discovered the conditions which explained this fact. By talking to their possible prospects they found that many Northwesterners had been badly deceived by another cream separator. That was why, when they advertised in the local farm journals, the farmers would not accept their claims. The manufacturers, located in the East, would never have guessed that they faced a different kind of a problem in Wisconsin and Michigan unless they had analyzed their prospects. After analysis they changed their tactics entirely; instead of advertising that their separator was cheaper than any other, they turned about and made the key-note of all their copy the fact that they would refund to the purchaser his money

ANALYSIS OF THE CONSUMER'S ATTITUDE 133

if the separator were not satisfactory. In that way they talked to the farmer in terms that conformed to his peculiar state of mind. They met his objection before he thought of it. His fear was eliminated by the money-back guarantee.

Analysis of consumer attitude is more important than analysis of conditions. A manufacturer of metal office furniture thought that people bought their steel office furniture through fear of fire. They made a research. Over 500 firms were written to, and 348 answered, giving their reasons for purchasing as follows:

```
Durability ............................... 25%
Fire protection........................... 16%
Appearance ............................... 14%
Convenience...............................  9%
Saving of space ..........................  8%
Impervious to climate ....................  7%
Sanitary qualities .......................  4%
```

A manufacturer of a cereal was not sure whether flavor, nourishment, convenience, or digestibility was his chief point of appeal, so he wrote to 500 users and personally put these questions to them.*

1. What brand of cereal do you usually use?
2. If your answer is our brand, please tell us: Why do you prefer our brand?
3. Have you ever used any other brand of cereal?
4. How was our brand first brought to your attention?
5. How often do you serve it in your home?
6. Do you serve it in any other way except as porridge?
7. If you gave up using our brand, why did you discontinue its use?
8. Why do you prefer the brand you are now using?

In almost everything there is a certain formula for success —a certain line of appeal which will win. Only analysis or experience can tell you what that secret is; and analysis is often cheaper than experience.

One man, as a result of intelligent analysis, was able to secure his inquiries on a certain article at a cost of 30 cents apiece; whereas another, with the same product, who failed to analyze his problem, had to pay over 60 cents apiece for his inquiry. The man who analyzed was able to make sales which amounted to about $30 each, at a cost of about $3 per sale; out of ten inquiries received at a cost of 30 cents each, he was able to sell one article.

The other man paid much more to effect a sale. When he spent $30 for a 6-inch "ad" in a certain publication, instead of getting 100 inquiries, as did the successful competitor, he got only 50 inquiries. This meant that he had paid about 60 cents for his inquiry. His selling expense was something like $12 on $30, instead of $6 on $30. He failed.

The secret which the successful man had discovered through analysis was that the article could not be sold entirely through advertising. He had found that a personal demonstration was necessary to make the prospect buy. He used his advertising simply to "sell" his descriptive "literature." The other man tried to sell the article in his advertisement instead of simply seeking to get an inquiry, which he could follow up with persuasive literature.

Analysis should also cover the matter of timeliness. In publication advertising, along in July and August, the space used is far less than that used at other times of the year, because at that time most people are away on vacations and, as a rule, do not buy as much as at other times of the year; so the average advertiser saves up his appropriation until people are more likely to be in the market for what he has to offer. But certain things can be advertised with more timeliness in summer than in other seasons. Obviously, a beverage ought to be advertised most heavily during July, August, and September. Rings and other jewelry may be most advantageously advertised in the Christmas season.

The manufacturer must ask: "Is this something I had better advertise twelve months of the year, or is it better to advertise it at intervals?" All such questions should be decided by an analysis of the element of timeliness. For instance, the manufacturer of a tasteless Castor-Oil thought that the summer-time was a good time for his product, be-

ANALYSIS OF THE CONSUMER'S ATTITUDE 135

cause the doctors said so. He planned to concentrate his advertising campaign in July or August. But he investigated the comparative demand in the drug-stores during those months and found that his advertising would pay better in the fall and winter.

In the automobile field this question of timeliness is somewhat baffling. Many say that the best time to advertise automobiles is in the summer, because then the desire for a car is keenest. Others say that those who are able to buy automobiles are away at that time, and that people do not read as much during the warm months as they do in the fall and winter. Several automobile manufacturers have sent out to all the owners of their products a long list of questions, in an effort to get the owners to say at what time of the year they are most likely to be interested in the question of a new car. Such analysis is expensive, but usually pays in the long run.

Advertising agencies have developed the science of analysis to a very high degree. Here, for instance, is the list of questions which one agency asks of each new advertiser prior to a thorough investigation of trade conditions, consumer attitude, and pertinent statistics.

A. *The Product—*
 1. What are the trade-names and trade-marks?
 2. What are the main divisions of products?
 3. What are their relative volumes of sales?
 4. Are products patented, and how do they compare in value with other brands?
 5. What technical or other advantages have they?
 6. From a manufacturing standpoint, which would be the most profitable product to concentrate upon?

B. *Consumption—*
 1. What is the total consumption of each division of product:
  (a) In the United States?
  (b) In each State?

(c) In cities and towns of 10,000 or over?
(d) In towns of 10,000 and under?
2. What is the consumption per capita?
3. What is the total possible consumption?
4. What is the average purchase by an individual consumer?
5. How many consumer purchases in a year?

C. *Competition*—
1. How many competitors are there, and what percentage of the total business has each competitor?
2. How many advertised brands are there? (a) What are their comparative prices? (b) The extent and type of their advertising? (c) Have they tried localized advertising plans?
3. What percentage of gross sales are competitors spending for their advertising?
4. What do their sales organizations consist of?
5. How many competitors have national and how many have restricted distribution?

D. *Distribution*—
1. What is your distribution?
   (a) How many branches—where?
   (b) What does sales organization consist of—salaried men—commission men?
2. How many possible dealer-customers have you (classified)?
3. To what extent do dealers influence consumer purchases?
4. How many different brands do dealers carry?
5. Do any jobbers handle the goods?
6. Are wholesale and retail prices fluctuating or fixed?
7. Are there any peaks and low spots in selling seasons? When?

ANALYSIS OF THE CONSUMER'S ATTITUDE

E. *Consumer—*
1. Which division of product would be easiest to sell to consumer?
2. Which division is purchased most by brand?
3. What is consumer's present attitude toward product?
4. Is it a necessity or luxury, and how long will it last?
5. Does its purchase involve a change in buying habit on the part of the consumer or the expenditure of money which would not otherwise be spent?
6. Which is main appeal:
   (a) Value.
   (b) Utility.
   (c) Pride.
   (d) Appearance.

CHAPTER XVIII

Methods of Distribution

The producer or wholesaler who seeks to sell more than locally must first decide how he is to distribute his goods. How to advertise them will depend entirely on which sales system he chooses. Sales systems are called method of distribution. Of these there are four main methods:
1. Through the mail direct to consumer.
2. Through retail branches direct to consumer.
3. Through jobbers through dealers to consumer.
4. Through wholesale branches through dealers to consumer.

For instance, suppose you make wire fence. You will have competitors in the national field who do not manufacture their own wire fence. They buy it from another factory. Your own and another concern may each do a business of $3,000,000 a year. Yet you may use an entirely different system of distribution.

You may dispose of your wire through a sales force. Perhaps you will have about fifty men—one man to a State. These men go through the country and call on the dealers. John Jones who runs the feed mill at Angola, for instance, will be called on by your representative, who will try to get Mr. Jones to buy your wire fence and pay for it on delivery. Eventually, John Jones, in turn, will sell your wire fence to the farmers in his surrounding territory and pocket a profit on each sale that he makes.

Your competitor may not nave a single salesman. Perhaps his only employees are his office force. He may use thousands of dollars' worth of advertising each year instead of a sales organization. He announces his wares in about one hundred and fifty different farm journals or agricultural

METHODS OF DISTRIBUTION

publications. These "ads" are simply designed to bring in inquiries. They say that "this is good fence, and it is only 23 cents a rod." The farmer is supposed to write in and say: "I would like more information. Send me your catalogue." Thus, without salesmen, this other man relies on the mail to dispose of as many dollars' worth of wire fence each year as you do.

There are many such cases in which two concerns in the same business operate under entirely different sales methods. And before you can think of advertising, you must solve the big problem, "What method of distribution shall I adopt?"

In the case cited above, you and your competitor have the same product and the same market. You each have wire fence to sell—and you each have the farmers to whom to sell your fence. The question is: How can you make the greatest profit—by selling through salesmen, through dealers, or by selling in the direct way, by means of the mail?

Many economists favor the direct method of distribution from the wholesaler (whether he be the manufacturer or the jobber) right straight to the consumer—the person that will ultimately use the goods. This method has gained much favor. Its advocates hold that it eliminates the middlemen, and results in economy of distribution. But in actual figures it involves a fairly high cost per sale, for it entails expensive and extensive correspondence. The usual cost of getting a single inquiry as a result of an advertisement is about $1. The actual cost of getting a single new customer averages about $10, as only about one out of ten inquirers ultimately buys. The manufacturer, therefore, who sells through the local dealer with the help of local advertising may actually undersell his direct-dealing competitor when all is said and done.

Certain goods can be sold successfully by mail, and certain goods cannot. For instance, it would be impossible for the Cudahy Packing Company to sell Dutch Cleanser by mail direct to the consumer. Although the housewife might buy a package to-day and another package next month, each package would mean only a 10-cent sale. The cost of selling—

the cost of all the necessary correspondence and other items—would more than wipe out all possible profit.

A 10-cent article of that kind would be impossible of sale by the direct-by-mail method. Even a 50-cent article would seldom permit the use of such a method. And yet, there are exceptions; some novelties, such as watch-fobs, may be sold by this method with fair success. If the fob brings 50 cents and costs, say 4 cents, the seller would have 46 cents gross profit, which might take care of the cost of getting the inquiry and might also cover the other expenses of letters and the follow-up literature necessary to complete the sale. But if that 50-cent article should cost the advertiser 30 cents, it would be impossible for him to market it successfully by the direct-by-mail method. On the other hand, if your product averages from $25 to $50 for each order, then even if each inquiry costs a dollar, and each sale costs $10, provided the margin of profit is large enough, the direct-by-mail method may be profitable and mail-order advertising may prove a gold-mine.

To sell successfully by mail another element is essential—to get repeat business. In other words, you must be fairly sure that your this-year customer, when he decides to use some more goods in your line two years from now, will buy from you, because, as a rule, a mail-order business cannot make profits unless the first selling expense of securing a customer is divided over many subsequent orders, which ultimately must come in from the person whom you win as a new patron; otherwise, the cost of the first sale is usually so high that you will lose money.

If you are selling a staple article, an article which most people want and use, you have got to sell on the basis of price if you use the mail-order method. Other things being equal, it is easier for the average person to call up the local store and say: "Send me so-and-so" than to go to the trouble of ordering goods by mail. People will not send to a distant city for their goods, rather than buy at home, unless they believe they can get those goods for less money—or unless they can get goods not locally available.

Mail-order advertising has progressed from an effort to use the space itself as a catalogue to one toward getting the reader to send for a catalogue.

The fact is, many, many millions have been lost in the chase for mail-order fortunes. Unless you have the resources to wait and wait you had better use the usual methods; and if your product and merchandise do not happen to suit the mail-order method, you cannot possibly succeed with that plan of distribution although you may win out handsomely in selling through dealers.

Let us suppose that you manufacture shoes and you select the mail-order plan of distribution. In advertising you ask people to order by mail. Can you market your shoes successfully in this way? If the public knows that your shoes are about the same as those they have bought at their department store at $7.50, and if you offer those shoes for $5.50—then, providing you prove you are reliable, people may send for your shoes because they know shoe values and can compare. But with goods, the value of which is not so obvious as in the case of shoes, you will find it more difficult to sell.

When it comes to intangible things like investment bonds, you cannot sell to the general public unless you explain the bonds to the prospects personally. Very few people outside of professional investors know just how much any certain kind of bond is worth. When you say in your "ad" that your bond offers a fine opportunity to make money, average people are not impressed. They are not able to say to themselves, as they might in the case of shoes or something else of known value: "This is worth so-and-so. At the price offered I can buy this to my profit."

Take an example: A factory which was doing a $300,000 business annually had been selling through the dealer at a minimum manufacturing profit. The dealer made a gross profit of $5 or more on each of their products. The manufacturer decided there was no reason why he could not pocket that $5 profit himself. And so, without further consideration, he embarked on a mail-order campaign. Of course, the first thing that happened was that his customers—the dealers—ceased buying from him. They were angry. They did not like to have the factory say to the people: "Don't buy from your local dealer—buy direct from the factory and save money." The manufacturer gave up all chance of regaining these retail dealers on whom he had spent so much time and money. He found that he could get some orders by mail—but not enough to pay for the cost of getting that business direct from the consumers. His success was further precluded by the fact that his product possessed no "repeat" quality. During a lifetime a person might buy two of his articles—at an interval of perhaps twenty years. Even when the manufacturer gained a customer at an expense of $5 or $6 worth of advertising and sales cost, he could not expect a second purchase for many years. The cost of securing a purchaser had to be absorbed in that first sale. Each sale amounted to less than $10. The gross profit was less than $5. The cost of getting the mail-order was over $5. The concern failed.

And yet, the Sears, Roebuck Company sells over $300,000,000 worth of goods every year. They sell 100,000 different articles to 6,000,000 customers. Ten years ago they were only a moderate success. Simply through cumulative ability to keep old customers and to get new ones, they have become the largest mercantile business in the world. But the keystone of their success has been their ability to offer low prices. They are able to buy in such quantity that they get their goods at rock-bottom cost. They sell on bargain appeals.

Successful mail-order houses answer requests with extraordinary rapidity: a catalogue is mailed the day the inquiry is received. Personality cannot enter into this kind of selling. The sales must be made simply on price and on service. Some mail-order men try to sell on personality. All their "ads" bustle with big "I's." With photographs of themselves they seek to instil personality into their advertising and hope that it will charm people into buying. But personality does not seem to act as well in mail-order distribution as do the elements of price and service.

Usually the big mail-order house has a diversity of merchandise. Sometimes, however, the business is concentrated along a single line, such as wearing apparel—especially suits, cloaks, coats, and goods of that kind. There is one company using the mail-order method which sells $50,000,000 worth of clothes every year. Many others in the same general line sell over a million dollars' worth a year in the same way.

These concerns sell simply by presenting a picture and a price. They make it easy for the prospect to sit down by the evening lamp and see what pretty clothes she can get for what seems to be so little money. Women think they know about this kind of merchandise. They think they understand clothing values. Therefore, they believe they can readily measure how much they will save. Consequently, they do not hesitate to buy by mail.

There are other kinds of mail-order successes. Instead of the appealing-by-price argument, some mail-order institutions, known as premium houses, offer savings in round-about ways. For instance, they say: "You would have to pay 5 cents for a cake of soap if you bought it at the corner grocery store. Buy it from us and we will give you 5 cents' worth of hairpins in addition." That is the principle of the premium system upon which this kind of mail-order house operates.

CHAPTER XIX

Retail Branches and Exclusive Agencies

Can the manufacturer or wholesaler straddle the distribution problem? Can he enjoy the long profit of the mail-order system and at the same time utilize dealer distribution? This dual method is seldom attempted—although there are examples of its successful application—for if a producer tries to go to the public through mail and thus cut out the dealer, the dealer is usually so antagonized that he refuses to buy from the producer.

A certain mattress manufacturer tried to make a success of dual distribution in this way: He sold his mattress by mail to the consumer for $20. He sold the same mattress to the dealer for $10. And the dealer was able to sell a great many mattresses as long as he could afford to sell them for $15, whereas the regular price advertised in the magazines was $20. But even at that the dealer did not like to sell this mattress. In many furniture stores throughout the country samples of it were kept in the back part of the shop. Dealers would open these up and show them to a customer to convince her that she should not buy this advertised mattress. They tried to prove that another mattress—which the customer could buy for $14—was just as good as the one which she had come in to buy at the price of $15.

The dual method is usually a dangerous system of distribution, as you can readily see. For instance, suppose you make furniture. There are 5,000 possible good dealers. Suppose each of them sells $1,000 worth of your goods each year. That means an annual volume of $5,000,000, and at the barest manufacturing profit this would be a highly lucrative business.

Now suppose you decide to sell some of your furniture by mail. An advertising appropriation of $50,000 may bring you 50,000 inquiries, if you are lucky; and if your luck continues you may sell to 10% of these inquirers. Suppose you sell to 5,000 customers. Their orders would not average $1,000, like those of the dealers. If they averaged $25, that would mean a total business of $125,000, and even if your profit were many times as large, you would not receive as much net income as from through-the-dealer distribution.

Some experts recommend the direct method at the start of a business. They argue that this quickens the distribution, so that later it is easy to enlist the dealers and adopt the ordinary system of dealer distribution; but if a manufacturer is advertising nationally while following this policy, each dollar so spent by him cannot be as effective as if his goods were on hand in the better stores throughout the nation.

The virtue of a direct-to-consumer system of distribution is that it makes possible a relationship with the ultimate users. When you sell through the local dealer he exercises control and the manufacturers are more or less at his mercy; but there is a way to deal with the consumer and yet get the extensive volume that comes from having your goods conveniently at hand so that the consumer does not have to buy by mail. This method is the direct-through-agents system. For instance, typewriters, as a rule, are sold direct to users through the manufacturers' own salesmen. If you are in the market for a certain brand, you can buy it in your town only at the company's local branch office. You must deal with the manufacturer's own salesman. This is natural, because in order to sell specialties of this kind a man must know a great deal about such machines—much more than he could possibly know if he were also selling bicycles and desks and other things. He has to be a specialty salesman. It is necessary for such manufacturers to have more than their advertising, more than the most powerful follow-up literature that man can create. They have to rely on the personality of especially trained salesmen, who are experts at selling their particular make of machine.

One large typewriter manufacturer who sought to change this method by adopting a mail-order plan found that a

Above, a recent magazine page. At left, an "ad" of twenty years ago. Here the improvement is in taste—in making the tradename more delicate and tempting, in filling the advertisement with human interest which, in turn, suggests pleasure, purity, and festivity. The Sampler, itself, gives an added attraction. Its success has been notable as a successful little device for strategic merchandising.

great cut in the price of the typewriter was necessary to make up for the lack of personal salesmanship.

Most automobile factories employ a similar system. Their advertising may establish a prejudice in favor of their car. They may also follow up with letter after letter. But in order to sell cars and get people to spend money which they otherwise would not spend, they must utilize specialized salesmen to complete the solicitation. These automobile salesmen must know automobiles and know them well.

Many shoes are sold by this same method. The very largest factories distribute their output through their own stores. They cannot sell by mail with much success. But in the direct-through-branch system, they do not have to rely on advertising alone. Their publicity need only establish that atmosphere which will make people want their goods; then the prospect will go to the store and the salesman completes the sale.

Sometimes producers have their own agents and their own retail stores, and also sell in practically every hamlet in the country wherever they can get a grocer or druggist or confectionery store to put their goods on the counter. This is the system of many of the big candy companies. They have their own stores in some places. In others they sell through the stores of the independent dealer.

If you, as a manufacturer, have your own retail branch in a certain town, the other dealers in that community will prefer not to compete at retail with you, the manufacturer. They are, therefore, unlikely to buy any goods from your factory.

Another question to be faced is whether you should appoint dealers as exclusive agents. Suppose that in a given locality, where you have no retail store of your own, there are two good stores. One is run by Frank Smith and the other by John Jones. Suppose your product is a certain kind of laundry soap. Your salesman goes to Smith and says: "We want you to be our exclusive agent in this town. We won't sell to Jones at all. If you teach your customers that our soap is best, they can't go to Jones for it, because Jones won't

RETAIL BRANCHES AND EXCLUSIVE AGENCIES 149

have it. So, you see, it will be worth your while to recommend and push my goods." That is the idea of the system of exclusive agencies by which you sell your goods to only one dealer in each locality. The objection to it is that when you go to Smith and sell him your soap and say that Jones can't have your soap, you decrease the amount that you can sell. Let us say that each dealer has 500 customers. You get only 500 possible prospects at Smith's store. The 500 customers who deal at Jones' are excluded as prospects; and yet, those 500 customers of your exclusive dealer may buy more soap than if both dealers handled it, for if Smith really pushes it, more people will buy it than if Jones sold your soap too.

Certain products have to be sold through exclusive agencies. Fine furniture—notably sectional bookcases—seem to be in this class. Each one of these lines has broad competition. Each of these manufacturers must fight competitors who seek to sell at lower prices. The personality of an intelligent salesman on the floor is needed to persuade people to pay the extra money that these goods cost.

As a rule the manufacturer who sells his goods through exclusive agencies does not try to use the exclusive system in a big city. Here the dealers are not in such personal competition with each other. In the small town, the dealers are likely to be fighting each other tooth and nail, so that if Smith handles your goods, Jones, for that reason, will not want to. A large city may be divided into distinctive sections, and it is often possible to have one "exclusive" dealer in each section; but, in general, the exclusive-agent plan works best in the smaller places.

CHAPTER XX

Producer—Jobber—Dealer Distribution

In the majority of cases the producer sells his goods to the jobber, who sells them to the retailer. Practically all groceries are sold by this method; practically all drugs. Hardware—particularly the smaller articles—is sold by this system. On all such items the dealer can save store space and other expenses by letting the jobber buy and carry his goods, which the dealer can order out as he needs them.

Suppose that you have a retail hardware business in a down-town location. If you were to carry in your store all the stock that you would have to buy in order to get quantity prices, you would probably need three times as much floor space. This would cost a tremendous amount of money. A wholesale store in a less expensive section can carry its stock so cheaply that the cost of goods, plus storage space, plus jobber's profit, usually totals less than the factory cost plus the cost of the retailer's more expensive floor space and other fixed charges.

In a through-the-jobber system it is more necessary than ever to create a consumer demand in order to make the goods flow from jobber, to retailer, to consumer. Take breakfast foods, for instance. Some cereal manufacturers seldom go near the retail dealer. They may advertise to him so that he will favor their product. But they do not call on the retail dealers. They feel that he will sell just as much as the public asks for—no more and no less. Nor do these manufacturers much concern themselves with the jobber.

By using jobbers, a manufacturer can do away with warehouses. He may also reduce the number of his customers; he may have one big account instead of hundreds of retail dealers. In return for this warehousing and bookkeep-

PRODUCER—JOBBER—DEALER DISTRIBUTION 151

ing function, the jobber usually gets about 15% discount. But the manufacturer must depend on publicity to create the flow of his goods, for the usual jobber's salesman takes orders for thousands of different items and cannot be expected to push any particular brand of goods unless it be the jobber's own brand.

Most producers depend on the jobber and the dealer merely for the performance of the mechanical function of stocking the goods. The selling of goods in the active sense is dependent on the advertising. In extreme instances this advertising must even make the consumers want the goods so keenly that they will force the dealers to carry them. The dealer then will force the jobber to keep them in stock for his convenience. In that way the jobber will be compelled to buy.

In this connection advertising performs its strongest function. It is the life-blood of this method of distribution. But even in this case it is wisest to cultivate the jobber and dealer. For in many instances it is possible for the dealer to shift the consumer's desire from your product, which the consumer asks for, to some other, on which the dealer may make a few cents more. If your article is liable to substitution you must pay a great deal of attention to the dealer.

Even in the exclusive-agency plan of distribution it is necessary to get the dealer to back up your goods enthusiastically. If he does not, you lose. It would be better, then, to have two different dealers in the town rather than only one. To make your exclusive-agency plan win out you must continually stimulate the dealer. This is usually accomplished through house organs and circular letters, and other direct-mail work in addition to the visits by personal salesmen.

Some manufacturers virtually finance the dealer. Particularly in exclusive-agency distribution, the manufacturer will say: "Here, you put my goods in your store. You won't run any risk. If you don't sell them, I will take them back. If you do sell them, you pay me such-and-such a price for such as you sell." That is what is known as "putting goods in on consignment." But where the manufacturer sells to all good dealers, the dealer takes all the risk. He is in business absolutely for himself. When he gets his goods from the manufacturer, the manufacturer ends his part of the transaction. The dealer then takes over the task of selling those goods. He sells them for whatever price he pleases and on whatever terms. The merchandise is the dealer's property, without a string of any kind. But from a manufacturer's standpoint, this kind of distribution must concern itself with the consumer, for few dealers will push your product. In order to create a demand that will make the consumer ask for your product you must advertise to the general public.

By selling your goods to every possible dealer you can get your product into the greatest possible number of stores, if your price is fair. If your possible territory is limited, this plan is still more desirable. Suppose, for instance, you put out a line of dining-room chairs. Freight rates are so fixed that if you are an Eastern manufacturer you cannot possibly sell any dining-room chairs in Nebraska, because you will have to charge the Nebraska dealer so much more for your chairs than does the Chicago manufacturer. You would have to add to your prices a considerable freight cost.

The manufacturer who sells through this every-dealer method, and does not advertise, must take the least possible profit. A dealer will not push your goods if all the other dealers handle them unless he can make more money on your goods, or unless there is a decided demand for them. Your soap, let us say, sells at 5 cents and costs the dealer 4 cents. Another soap costs the dealer 3 cents, and that, too, sells for 5 cents. The usual dealer will sell the 3-cent soap whenever he can, because then instead of making 1 cent he would make 2 cents on each bar.

Low price is almost the only factor that will tempt a dealer to sell a lot of your goods if you do not enlist him in active support by granting him an exclusive agency—or if you do not force him through advertising. If you sell the dealer on a price-basis that will give him an extra large margin—even if you cut your profit to the very bone—it is likely that a competitor may cut under you. Then your business will slide away unless you, in turn, go under him. That will

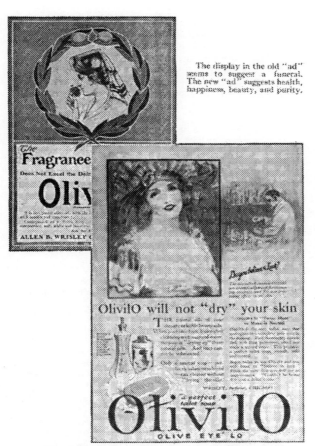

At left, an advertisement of 1900. Below, a recent magazine page. Note that for twenty years, the name has carried an explanation of its pronunciation.

either force you to inferior quality of product, or heavy losses and possibly ultimate failure.

On the other hand, if you give the dealer a fair margin, and cause him to sell your goods by making the public buy them from him, then you are constantly building up an indestructible asset of good-will and certain business progress. To create such a demand, advertising is needed. This advertising will insure you a fair manufacturing profit—will quicken the dealer's turnover—and will also protect the consuming public against any letting down of quality.

This quickening of turnover is a vital point. Many, many dealers are looking less for long margins of profit and more for fast-moving advertised products. This is because live merchants are seeing the truth of the principle that net profit comes from volume of business. That is why the usual salesman selling advertised goods puts his emphasis upon the advertising behind them even more than upon the intrinsic merit of his goods. For instance, the successful salesman of to-day is likely to persuade his dealer prospect with the following line of salesmanship:

"Now and then you have stocked goods, and they stayed on your shelves and you had to take a loss on them. Do you know why they did not move? Wasn't it because they were not advertised heavily enough? Or, if they were advertised heavily enough, wasn't it because they didn't have the quality—the quality that insures repeat-sales?

"If you were told that a certain brand of preserves was to be advertised heavily week in and week out, in all the local newspapers in big space—and in full showing on the biggest twenty-four sheet poster boards and in any other ways—wouldn't you stock up on that preserve? Probably you would even though it required an investment on your part of many dollars.

"And, if the advertising were strong enough, and if the preserves were good enough, they would move out of your store quickly and you would make money on them.

"You have more advertising behind my goods than on any other similar article in your store. Think that over—it is the great big point that has much to do with the profit of your business. What this means to your turnover is startling, if you will but figure it out. Suppose you carry a stock of $10,000 worth of goods altogether. Suppose you do a business of $50,000 per year.

"That will mean that you will turn over your entire stock on an average of five times per year. Your fixed costs of doing business are probably around 25%. In other words, on $50,000 worth of business, your rent, light, heat, and pay-roll, and other items of overhead, ought to equal about $12,500. If you turned over your stock ten times per year instead of five times per year, it would mean that you would be doing $100,000 worth of business instead of $50,000 worth of business annually.

"And your light, heat, rent, etc., would probably not increase very much. The result would be a profit of about 5% on your first $50,000 worth of business and a possible profit of 20% on the additional $50,000 worth of business—if you could only turn over your stock ten times instead of five times. You can double your turnover if you carry our advertised goods. It is the great advertising behind them that will enable you to do this. The fact that you ought to have enough stock on hand to more than meet that demand is an axiom. It is as obvious and certain as the fact that one and one make two. And remember this about our advertising. It doesn't go up like a sky-rocket and then fall like a stick. In fact, it never stops. It never stops—that is the nub of our policy both as to advertising and quality."

CHAPTER XXI

Consumer Advertising which Enlists the Dealer

Although more and more dealers are seeing the advantage of handling advertised brands, it is still necessary to plan most consumer-advertising campaigns with one eye on the dealer. Of course, the purpose of most advertising is to make consumers want the advertised product. But in some cases the consumers do not buy what is advertised even though they have decided that they want it.

The dealer is often the making, or breaking, of an advertising-selling campaign. The word "advertising-selling" is used purposely, because an advertising campaign must sell goods, and no advertising campaign succeeds unless the dealers have been "sold"—which means more than the mere securing of distribution. "Selling the dealer" must go beyond putting the goods on his shelf. Most of us who have actually sold goods on the road know that the dealer makes the majority of decisions as to what brand of the desired kind of goods his customers will buy. And yet the dealer wants goods that will sell. He knows that the main power that will make the goods sell is advertising. "Are these goods going to move?" That is as big a question in the live dealer's mind as: "Are they of good quality?"

The dealer must therefore know that you are advertising, and how you are advertising. To illustrate this point, take some of the methods which have been found successful in putting across consumer advertising that enlists the dealer. The obvious and simplest means of causing consumer advertising to influence the dealer is to advise the dealer of the advertising by means of a mailing campaign.

In marketing a new cracker, the way was paved for the salesmen, and the dealer was enlisted, by taking the first five

ADVERTISING WHICH ENLISTS THE DEALER 157

"ads" of the campaign and printing them on five different government post-cards, with the name of the product omitted. These were mailed to each dealer in the territory where the advertising was to be done.

Every other day the dealer received one of these "teaser" post-cards. They suggested that this was just what father, mother, sister, brother wanted, and would buy from him. Of course, a little curiosity was excited. Then, ten days later, the solution to the puzzle arrived in the form of a proof of the big newspaper "ad," containing all the previous pieces of copy together with the name of the new product. By this time the dealer was pretty well acquainted with the cracker, and realized that it was going to be advertised. The salesman, who came along a few days later, found that the dealer was already sold, and it was almost a matter of simply taking his order.

For three years a company manufacturing a patented specialty had been spending thousands of dollars to get a foothold. The commodity was so intricate that it could not be described in type and illustration. Its desirability had to be demonstrated. After six months' work a moving sign was designed and placed in a 5-and-10-cent store during the summer months. It worked! Many of these signs were put into the windows of the most desirable dealers—dealers who had seen the virtue of the commodity and had stocked up well, but had found that the goods would not move. Take this as an illustration of the value of this kind of hooking-up of the dealer: A salesman went to New York. In the Hudson Terminal Building there was a big store. The salesman offered this dealer a sign if he would buy a gross of the specialty.

"Why," replied the dealer, laughing in the salesman's face —"I wouldn't buy those things unless I knew they were going to sell—and as to your putting that moving sign in my window, you'll have to pay rental for the space it takes."

But finally that dealer was persuaded to try it out. A year later the manufacturer tried to get that dealer to release the sign so that they could put it in another dealer's window. He refused! Good orders from that store are now coming in every month. And this manufacturer, in general, as a result of hooking-up the dealer with the consumer-advertising, is to-day doing in one month the amount of business that he was able to do during the entire third year of his existence.

The angle of the "copy" itself may often mean the enlistment of the dealer. In starting the advertising of a new food product a large "ad" showed a fine-looking grocer holding out a package. The dealers were so pleased with this idealized presentation of their side of the merchandising that many were willing to paste clippings of these "ads" on their windows. And the "ads" that followed for the next two months kept featuring the dealer. One of them showed a sign containing the name of the product, with the dealer pointing to it. The caption was: "By this sign ye shall know good grocers." As a result of this kind of advertising this brand was quickly placed in thousands of stores.

The same method has helped a grocery specialty. This was well established, was enjoying a fair increase, but in a certain territory for many reasons it had slumped. Investigators went through this field, spending three days in a big city and two days in the neighboring villages. They found that the dealers were simply apathetic. The specialty had become an old story with them. There was a fair demand for it, but their love had gone elsewhere.

As a result of this investigation the campaign was pushed on a new line. Newspapers were necessarily the medium, as the distribution was limited to five states. The manufacturer wrote to every dealer that had ever bought this product and enclosed a list of the newspapers in which the big "ads" were to be run. A government post-card was enclosed, on which the dealer was asked to state in which of those papers he wished his name to appear. At the bottom of this post-card there were three blank lines where the dealer could write an order if he wished. The week following the sending out of these letters brought in thousands of these post-cards. Many of these carried orders aggregating thousands of dollars.

The "ad" on top was published in 1900. The large "ad" is of recent date. The point of progress is the latter's reason-why appeal—"50% cheaper than paint."

But of course the main function that this mailing performed was to make the dealer realize that the product was to be advertised, and make him realize that fact in a clearer and more personal way than could be accomplished by any other method.

When the dealer is an exclusive dealer, handling a product which involves a large amount per sale, it is possible to use an almost perfect form of the kind of "consumer-advertising-that-enlists-the-dealer." By this plan the manufacturer goes 50–50 on advertising done in the dealer's locality, over the dealer's name. This idea works out well. Usually the dealer is enthused, as well as aided, by this sharing of local advertising expense.

Some manufacturers have gone farther in an effort to inspire dealers by practically taking them into partnership in the advertising problem. Before making a definite appropriation they have corresponded with each dealer—talking over the situation in his city—getting him to recommend his choice of paper—discussing with him the amount of money it would take, and agreeing that (if he would share the expense 50–50) they would put that item for his city into the factory advertising appropriation. And the copy was built in a way that made it seem like the dealer's own advertising. The "ads" lacked all "factory" flavor, and instead were the straight, plain merchandising "ads" which the dealer wanted for the quick turn-over of his goods.

A good time to enlist the dealer is before a new article is started. In introducing a new toilet preparation the makers were not sure which of two main virtues would prove to be the greatest talking point in the advertising and selling of the product. Briefly, they put the question up to the dealers by mail. They got 68% replies. Practically all of them agreed. In this way they found out what was the cardinal selling-point, and also they got the dealer's keen preliminary interest in the article prior to the time it was offered to him.

Consumer-advertising-that-enlists-the-dealer can be accomplished through more ways than dealer-signs and newspapers and direct by mail. Successful plans for using the same system have been worked out through the medium of the painted bulletin. And through the magazines this principle of advertising is sometimes magically successful. For instance, in advertising an expensive machine an advertiser took a page in a leading magazine, left about one-third of the page blank at the bottom, and sent proofs to certain dealers whom he especially wanted in certain cities. He advised them that the names of all dealers would be listed in this space, and asked them to authorize him to list their name, so that the inquiries which emanated from that community could be referred to them.

In order to secure a dealership in this way it was necessary for the dealer to order a sample totalling over $1,000 net cost. Six such applications and orders came in by telegram. The business done by that advertisement paid for itself many, many times over. The actual space used by the list of dealers' names did not hurt the persuasive power of the appeal in general. Instead, in the main, it helped it to win out.

The most usual method is to ignore the dealer and to force dealer distribution through advertising to the consumer. By this method you seek to advertise your soap, for instance, so heavily as to create a demand which would make the dealer sell your product whether he makes 1 cent per cake, or whether he makes 1½ cents per cake. Such a campaign requires tremendous resources. During the first two or three years, you will probably not net enough profit to pay for that advertising. Your profit will come from the cumulative demand—the snow-ball-like building up of your business which will result from the fact that a first trial will so satisfy each new user that she will buy more, and will tell her friends.

CHAPTER XXII

Advertising—Plus Sales Work

The aim of an advertising campaign is to sell the greatest possible amount of goods. To do that it is necessary to create the greatest possible demand on the part of the consumers. But your campaign will fall flat if you do not take care of the other factors which facilitate the fulfilment of the demand thus created. No matter how heavily you advertise, little will come of your work if, in the meantime, you do not build up your machinery of distribution. The jobber should have your goods in his warehouse ready to let the dealer have a stock before the consumer goes to the dealer and asks for your brand.

Suppose you adopt a campaign which calls for full pages in national weeklies, or large space in general magazines, or extensive use of street-car cards. Then you may gather your sales organization and say: "We shall start to manufacture 'such-and-such' soap next month. We shall advertise it heavily. Most people will want so good a soap at so low a price. We shall tell the public about it in this strong way. So you go out and stock the dealers."

Your salesman goes out. He has copies of the proposed "ads." He approaches the dealer in some such way as this: "Here's our new soap. You get it for 3½ cents a cake and sell it for 5 cents. That means a good profit for you. Moreover, you are going to sell a great deal of it as a result of all this advertising we are going to do. Many people will come in and ask for the soap. Better take a couple of gross."

The dealer gives him an order. Then the salesman sees the other dealers. At the end of a week he may have about fifty gross on his order-book. Then he goes to the jobber in that particular section and tells him what he has done. The jobber offers to take over the orders for these local dealers. He also orders an additional number of gross, in the expectation that the dealers will want more as soon as the advertising begins to pull the soap off their shelves.

This system of distribution in advance of demand is the most logical. But unfortunately, or perhaps fortunately, a good many of those promised avalanches of demand never come. Many a dealer who puts a gross in his store finds that the advertising causes hardly a dozen or so to move. He takes his medicine. But when another salesman comes around with a similar proposition he is likely to say: "Well, I will take a dozen, and if it goes the first day or so I can get another dozen from my jobber." This method by which the dealer puts in a minimum stock is probably best for him, and, in the long run, is probably best for the advertiser.

The dealer of to-day can pretty well estimate how much demand there will be on the basis of a certain advertising proposition. Anyway, he knows that most of the goods which are advertised can easily be secured from his jobber. In an effort to overcome this tendency, by which the dealer buys sparingly, some manufacturers have abused advertising by tempting the dealer to overstock. The salesman is likely to say: "If you buy a gross from me now, I will put in an extra dozen free." That is called a "free deal." The purpose is to make the dealer fill his shelves so that he will put all his effort into getting rid of the goods, and in that way positively co-operate. But as a rule, this turns out otherwise. The dealer soon forgets that he got an extra dozen by buying a large quantity. He remembers that he has all those goods on his shelves and that they decrease in value every minute they grow dirtier and staler. Therefore, he forms a prejudice. He is likely to get angry at this merchandise and close it out at a cut price. Then, in the future, he will try to sell a competitor's brand instead.

But it is highly dangerous to run your advertising without first making sure that the consumers can get your goods from the dealer when they ask for them. If the dealer has to say that he does not have your advertised soap, the consumer will seldom take the trouble to try elsewhere. Even if the dealer has twenty calls, he may then ask his jobber for only half a dozen, or as few as he can get along with.

The method of letting distribution follow the creation of demand is often of tremendous wastefulness. Suppose, for instance, that you are spending $5,000 for a page in a national periodical. Suppose in a town of ten thousand there are five hundred people who read that publication. Suppose fifty of these who see your advertisement are persuaded to go to John Smith, grocer, for your product. If they decide to do that, they will probably go there the day after they see your "ad." If Smith does not have your soap the consumer is likely to say: "All right, give me the usual kind." And next week, when the dealer has your soap, Mrs. Consumer will have forgotten your "ad." Therefore most of the money you spend in that magazine, in order to get those fifty people to go to that store, will be wasted unless the local dealer is stocked.

One of the safest and surest ways to secure distribution is to get your goods into a dealer's store on the promise that you will use newspaper space in his town, in addition to your national advertising. If you use this system—town by town and state by state—you can eventually cover the country. This method is thorough but slow and expensive. It works because the dealer becomes personally bound up to your goods. He will be committed to your brand as a result of your advertising in his own local newspaper over his name. These factors will tend to make him co-operate for the sale of your goods. Then your appropriation in the broad general mediums will be more likely to have the maximum effect.

There are three principal methods of using local advertising to enlist the dealer and to insure distribution:

1. Without listing any dealers' names.
2. Listing names of all dealers in each piece of copy.
3. Using smaller "ads" over the name of one dealer at a time.

At left, a Libby "ad" of twenty years ago. Below, a recent page.

The old "ad" advertises a generality—a line of foods. The modern "ad" advertises a concrete thing and one thing only—apple butter. Which whets the appetite the more?

A SHORT COURSE IN ADVERTISING

Another method, and possibly the best of all, is to include in the local newspaper schedule one full-page advertisement in which dealers' names are to be listed. These full pages are merchandised in advance of their publication. The salesmen are furnished with copies which they show to the dealers, promising to feature all co-operating dealers by printing their names and addresses in the full pages. Then other "ads" follow, without any dealers' names. This plan is usually called the "page-merchandising plan." It has seldom been known to fail. It has been used on almost every variety of merchandise. It almost invariably gets maximum results with smallest expenditure of time, energy, and money.

Here is an outline of a typical plan of this kind:

May 3. Address to salesmen—outlining purpose of campaign, giving details. Presentation of portfolio containing proofs of advertising, photographs of window-trim material, etc., to be used by salesmen in calling on trade.

May 10. Letter from newspaper to entire trade in local territory—announcing campaign—advising dealers to co-operate—mentioning that dealer's name and address will appear in full-page advertisement without charge to dealer—enclosing government post-card on which dealer may designate how he wishes name and address to appear.

May 11. Salesmen start active sales endeavor—also canvass trade for name and address for ad—emphasizing big thing that the house is doing in this campaign to help the dealer.

May 17. Letter from newspaper to entire trade announcing Window-Display Contest during weeks of June 7 to June 26. Prizes to be awarded by advertiser. Securing of entrants—details of contest, etc., to be handled by Board of Judges. Photographs to be taken of window displays at expense of advertiser.

May 31. Newspaper communicates with dealers who have not signified their intention to co-operate either by letter or telephone. Notifying laggard dealers that noon, June 3, is the dead-line for accepting the offer to list name. Final appeal.
June 4. Final approval of dealers' name list.
June 7. Monday full page appears with dealers' names.
June 8. Tuesday, one-half page.
June 9. Wednesday, one-third page.
June 13. Sunday, one-half page.
June 15. Tuesday, one-fifth page.
June 16. Wednesday, one-fifth page.
June 20. Sunday, one-third page.
June 22. Tuesday, one-sixth page.
June 23. Wednesday, full page.
June 30. Announcement by newspapers of winners in Window-Display Contest, by letter to entire trade.
July 6. Letter to co-operating dealers by the advertiser, thanking them for their co-operation—suggesting that dealer will find it profitable to continue efforts on this line—calling attention to national advertising, etc.

This plan resulted in securing the co-operation of 323 dealers out of 400, in a community of less than a million—including a radius of 50 miles around the city itself. Over 250 window displays resulted.

Many advertisers have relied solely on local advertising to get their distribution built up, step by step. They are content to develop their market gradually, with local advertising. Then, as fast as they make one territory profitable, they use that sales income to start a harvest in another field. Meanwhile they keep their first soil well fertilized with continued publicity. They feel that this method is far better than the old system of persuading dealers to stock up through the promise of general national advertising. But the latter method of forcing distribution by blanketing the nation with periodical advertising is still the favorite. In the long run such a method usually wins out handsomely, although the first few years may require an advertising expenditure far greater than the sales income.

CHAPTER XXIII

The Salesman and the Advertising

In a general, through-the-dealer plan of national distribution, the question of sales organization is of prime importance. You must find out how to distribute your goods so as to have them on hand for the consumers when your advertising creates a demand. You must decide on your sales plan before you decide your questions of medium, or copy, or any of the other advertising details.

Some of the biggest successes in advertising have been largely due to the efficiency of sales organization. Salesmen find it even more and more important to know advertising. Many men in advertising positions to-day are former salesmen. One function of the man in the field selling goods is to make the dealer understand advertising, so that he will know why the advertised article will be better for him to sell than one which is not advertised. The salesman, in such cases, lifts his argument above mere quality and price, and makes the profit-to-the-dealer paramount. This, in turn, involves the question of the advertising's effectiveness as applied to the dealer's interest.

In advertising campaigns where it is hard to get the coöperation of the dealers, the manufacturer must train his salesmen in the principles of advertising. The salesman should help, personally, to make the advertising effective. Conversely, advertising is the salesman's best friend. As a stimulus to salesmen there is no greater force than the power of advertising, for with advertising the salesman has something more to offer than simply the goods and the price. He can also offer some real help by way of advertising aid; and the broad-minded dealer is more interested in the possibilities of his advertising than any other phase of his business program.

Without advertising, the salesman can discuss only those

things which have to do with his (the seller's) side of the fence. These considerations are all in terms of "me" and "us," so they do not appeal to the ego of the dealer. But the salesman who sells on the basis of the advertisedness of his goods talks in terms of the dealer's profit. As a result, his persuasion is on the dealer's side of the fence. He talks to the dealer in terms of "you" and "your" rather than of "me" and "our."

So the salesman who sells on the basis of advertising, helps himself most and also helps the dealer most. If the salesman knows the rudiments of advertising in a way that enables him to advise the dealer, he is exceptional. He is the man that the dealer is glad to see. The dealer cannot help but feel that such a salesman is thinking of his (the dealer's) profit. Therefore this type of traveller is more likely to sell to a dealer than if the atmosphere were pervaded with the "me" and "our" of the manufacturer.

Advertising needs this co-operation on the part of the sales organization. Many failures can be traced to the lack of it. If a sales organization does not hitch up to a publicity campaign, the advertising may not pay. But there is also a danger that the sales organization may overestimate the ability of the advertising to sell goods. In the old days when national advertising first began to hold sway, salesmen would exhibit great portfolios showing the front pages of a number of magazines to prove the immensity of combined circulation, and showing pictures of the "ads" which were to run. The salesman would display this in front of the dealer with the assertion that this meant a landslide of demand. The dealer would not know. He might be overcome by the mystery of this thing called advertising, a new element to both the salesman and dealer. But advertising is better understood by the salesman of to-day. He knows that it is more likely to create "acceptability" than "demand," in the literal sense. He knows that if the dealer gives an advertised brand a fair chance it will sell, whereas it will not sell if the dealer tries not to sell it.

The alert manufacturers are spending much time and ef-

On left, a Bauer & Black "ad" of twenty years ago. Below, a recent B. & B. announcement.

Never a corn
on millions of feet nowadays

Do you know that millions of people who use Blue-jay keep entirely free from corns?

If a corn appears it is ended by a touch. A Blue-jay plaster or a drop of liquid Blue-jay is applied.

The corn pain stops. Soon the whole corn loosens and comes out.

The method is scientific. It is gentle, easy, sure. Old-time harsh treatments are supplanted by it with everyone who knows it.

It is made by a world-famed laboratory, which every physician respects.

It is now applied to some 20 million corns a year. You can see that corn troubles are fast disappearing.

Then why pare corns and keep them? Why use methods which are out of date?

Try this new-day method. See what it does to one corn. You will never forget its quick and gentle action. Your druggist sells Blue-jay.

B&B Blue-jay
Plaster or Liquid
The Scientific Corn Ender
BAUER & BLACK Chicago New York Toronto
Makers of Sterile Surgical Dressings and Allied Products

This illustrates the value of simplicity—of advertising just one product at a time.

fort in impressing their salesmen with the power of advertising and in teaching them how to express the advertisability as well as the other qualities of the goods. This, for instance, is the way Mr. H. W. Alexander presented the case of advertising to his salesmen:

"There are ten reasons why you will gain by using advertising in your work. Here they are:

1. *Because* you are selling the house, and when you sell the house, you naturally sell all that it stands for—sound financial strength, supreme quality of merchandise, and the heaviest advertising of any concern in the field. All of this makes it easier for you to sell the line as a whole, where simply merchandise talk tends to sell individual items only.
2. *Because* the salesman to-day who talks advertising stamps himself as a man of modern ideas and a live wire. Since 22,000,000 people bought Liberty Bonds, since the Red Cross collected over $100,000,000 with the aid of advertising, people everywhere have a new conception of this great force and what it will accomplish. To none is this fact more illuminating than the retail merchant.
3. *Because* the advertising is working for you while you are calling on other dealers. That is why it will pay you to see that window cut-outs are being used; to keep the art-glass signs on the counters and on the shelves; to aid and urge dealers to use the cuts we supply for their local-newspaper advertising.
4. *Because* advertising is a market-maker. If the dealer has a market and a profit he can have no quarrel with the cost of the goods. The advertising makes the merchandise sell—the dealer makes money—you sell with less argument and discussion as to price.
5. *Because* both retailers and clerks are more interested in advertised than non-advertised lines. They will talk them stronger, push them harder. Never neglect an opportunity to tell both the advertising and merchandise features to clerks wherever possible.

THE SALESMAN AND THE ADVERTISING 173

6. *Because* you can show a dealer that a stock of advertised goods is always worth par. If he ever wants to sell out, which can he sell easier and get most for —a stock of standardized, nationally-advertised goods, or a collection of unknown, unbranded merchandise? By carrying nationally-advertised goods it is always possible to fill in a complete stock. Odd lines, miscellaneous brands, are like a four-flush—you can't fill to 'em.
7. *Because*, when you put your line of advertised goods into a merchant's store, you are building on something bigger than the dealer's own personality. Should the dealer die, resign, or sell out you are not so subject to the whims of the new buyer.
8. *Because*, likewise, you do not have to depend entirely upon your own personality. No salesman can be a hero to every dealer. With our advertising story to tell, every salesman has a far better chance of getting the line in.
9. *Because*, after you have sold a merchant, you can visit the local newspaper and get the publisher or advertising manager to follow up the merchant. Explain to the newspaper that the merchant should be running advertisements featuring our line at the same time our national advertising is appearing. You will usually get good co-operation there, and thus you leave this strong local force working for you after you are gone.
10. *Because*, when you have a dealer sold on advertising, you couple up with the efforts of a powerful Advertising Department at home that will be working with you and for you 365 days in the year. While you are travelling in other territory this department will be keeping up your fences, backing up your work, helping the dealer move his goods—holding his interest until you call the next time.

CHAPTER XXIV

Planning a General Campaign

You have perfected your product. You have settled your manufacturing problems. You have decided on your method of distribution. You have trained your sales organization. After all those big details are settled you are at last ready to start on the advertising details. If yours is a large organization you have an advertising manager. He has studied your distribution. He has worked with your sales manager to find out from the salesmen what sort of competition you are up against, what the market is, and what are the possibilities of repeat sales on your goods. After you have digested these different details of your market you can decide what kind of campaign will best fit the conditions which surround your particular problem.

At this point you will probably call in an advertising agency. You will tell these advertising agents that you have decided to spend, say $100,000 the first year in an advertising campaign to create a demand for your product. Meanwhile, your advertising manager has probably conceived a certain plan. The agents look over this plan. Undoubtedly they suggest changes. They offer amendments based on their experience with other articles, whether similar or otherwise. And then, after all the details of analysis have been settled, you authorize your agency to begin to place your contracts.

For instance, suppose you have decided to spend $50,000 in street-car cards, and $50,000 in newspapers, to comprise 100 different newspapers—an average of $500 each. The agency will make contracts with those newspapers in your behalf. They agree to use in your behalf so many inches of space in each town. They also make contracts with the street-railway advertising companies for a certain number of cards in these certain towns.

PLANNING A GENERAL CAMPAIGN 175

If you were to go to these newspapers direct and buy $50,000 worth of space it would cost you $50,000 anyway, and to make these contracts would take a lot of your time. A recognized agency, however, is allowed from 10% to 15% commission by the newspapers on all out-of-town business secured by the agency. That is where the agency gets its pay. Therefore, as a rule you can get, without extra expense, the service of an agency which would give you their counsel in building your plan and their aid in preparing your copy and art work, as well as all the clerical labor involved. All this would not cost you a cent more than if you were to try to place your advertising direct.

So your advertising manager decides, in conference with your agency, on the best course of action. Together they arrange the dates for insertion of the advertisements. If your advertising manager simply had to take care of the creation of these few advertisements in connection with this single campaign there would not be much need of an advertising department. But he has to do much more than that. He has to get out booklets and other follow-up literature—because these advertisements that are to run in the newspapers may carry coupons—so that the readers who are interested in your announcement may write to you and ask for more information. You may have to send them a little sample and a booklet which will tell why they should buy your product. And so, in this creation of booklets and in the execution of this system of taking care of inquiries and sending out that literature and those samples, your advertising department will have a tremendous amount of detail to attend to. In these matters you cannot expect the agency to help much, except by way of advice and counsel.

Then, too, the advertising department usually takes care of all the details of the direct advertising to the trade. This work with the dealer must be done. You must realize from the first that you are not the only manufacturer in your line. You have competition not only for the favor of the public, but also for fair treatment by the dealer. You have to cater to him. You have to prove to him that your goods are worth his support. Here enters a vast field of advertising mediums known as the trade publications. There are more than 1,000 important periodicals in trade journalism. Almost every single trade in the country, from tobacco through to lumber, has one or many such organs. These deal directly with the problems of the trade that they serve, and are usually read rather religiously by the dealer, although often there are so many such publications that the dealer does not read them as thoroughly as he would like to. Still, these trade journals are purely business propositions with the dealer. He feels justified in taking the time to go through them. To get the dealer's interest, therefore, and co-operation in support of your advertising efforts, these trade journals offer you a good opportunity for reaching your dealer-customers.

The trade journal, as a rule, is confidential to its own trade. The public knows nothing of it and is supposed not to see its contents. You can therefore tell the dealer in the trade journal how much he can make on every bar of your soap he sells. That, of course, is a mighty good argument why the dealer should sell it, but is a poor argument why the public should buy it. But above all, these trade journals are valuable in building up that spirit of co-operation which you need to help back up your other advertising.

Of course there are objections to trade publications. For one thing their cost is high compared to their circulations. Then, too, they are likely to be so crowded with advertising that even though you have a full page your "ad" may be lost. Possibly your advertising department may decide that the trade journals are not, of themselves, sufficiently strong in their ability to carry your message to the dealer, for the journals in some trades are stronger than in others. Then you would have to go to the dealer through an entirely different system. You may decide to send out a letter every week. You may decide to send a telegram now and then. Or, perhaps once a month you will publish a house organ and send it to the dealers.

One big national advertiser has a house organ which is almost a magazine. This goes to thousands of automobile

At lower left, an "ad" of 1900. Above, a modern page concerning which Paul V. Barrett, assistant advertising manager, says: "This is one of the most successful pieces of copy ever used by the Schools."

owners, but is mainly meant for a selected list of twenty thousand automobile dealers. This publication costs $50,000 a year; but it hammers home this manufacturer's argument to those twenty thousand dealers, month in and month out.

This magazine talks in the terms of the layman—the man on the other side of the fence. It explains the most technical engineering points in the simplest words. Any one can understand. Their message is untechnical, and yet the magazine is talking to men who are supposed to know automotive engineering. The advertising department of this factory pays more attention to that house organ than to their expenditure of three times as much money in the magazines and other mediums. They feel that the education of the dealer in their favor is the crucial point of their campaign.

And that is only one of many instances where the manufacturer finds it worth while to carry on two interrelated advertising campaigns—one to win the consumer, and the other to enlist the trade. In general, comprehensiveness is one of the great virtues of an advertising plan. The following example shows the general form of the usual national advertising plan. (To this, of course, there would be appended an itemized schedule and estimate of cost, plus a plan for inspiring the salesmen):

Plan of Campaign Summer and Fall

Because your product is used exclusively in the home the influence of women for or against its purchase is increasingly great.

That is why we recommend a campaign in the *Ladies' Home Journal*.

The *Ladies' Home Journal* campaign should include:

1. Three full pages in *Ladies' Home Journal* in July, September, and November.
2. A consumer folder on each "ad," appealing specially to women.
3. Three broadsides to dealers.
4. Three broadsides to dressmakers.

PLANNING A GENERAL CAMPAIGN

The farm field will undoubtedly be the next big market for you, and once the farmer's wife starts to use your product, the business will come with increasing rapidity.

There is enough potential business among farmers' wives to keep every manufacturer in your line busy for the next five years.

A special farm campaign in the *Farm Journal* is, therefore, recommended.

The farm campaign should include:

1. Four pages in the *Farm Journal* in June, August, October, and December. Special farm copy should be used.
2. A consumer folder on each "ad"—each folder showing the many uses of your product on the part of the farmer's wife.
3. Three broadsides for dealers showing them how to go after farm business and cash in on the campaigns.
4. A series of special rural "ads" for dealers' use in local papers.

The *Literary Digest* and *American Magazine* pretty nearly blanket the best homes of the country.

We suggest adding four pages in the *Digest* and in the *American Magazine* in July, September, October, and November.

The *Digest-American Magazine* campaign would include:

1. Five pages in *Literary Digest* (May to October inclusive).
2. Four pages in *American Magazine*.
3. Four broadsides to dealers.
4. Five consumer folders, based on the five "ads."
5. Five pieces of newspaper copy for dealers' use.

THE CAMPAIGN IN TRADE PAPERS

During the campaign the copy in dry-goods papers should have a distinct tie-up with the magazine copy. You must drive home this desirability of your goods in terms of profit for the dealer.

In dressmaking papers we should use one or two double spreads to put over the idea of the greatest campaign in your entire history.

KEEPING IN READINESS FOR NEWSPAPER DRIVE

Just the moment that production will permit it, a series of local drives in newspapers should be launched.

This campaign should be prepared almost immediately, perfected, and held in readiness so that on ten days' notice a drive can be launched.

THE BIG PORTFOLIO

This is the one big "smash" which will wake up your entire organization of jobbers, dealers, and salesmen. This book should show actual reproductions of all the publication advertisements, plus inspirational "trade" copy, plus figures showing in graphic form the width and depth of the circulation of each medium to be used.

On account of the expense we do not recommend that this be mailed to a big general list, although the result would probably justify even that.

The portfolio can be supplemented with broadsides which will cover the same ground in a less expensive way.

CHAPTER XXV
Continuity Through a Central Thought

There is a decided tendency in national advertising toward planning advertising in units of *campaigns*, rather than in units of individual advertisements, and of running a single idea as a definite thread throughout a whole series of advertisements which may comprise one or several campaigns. This method is based on what is variously called a "dominating idea," "scheme," "central thought," "running theme," and by other similar terms. The words "central thought" seem best to express the gist of the plan. The principle is that when a series of advertisements is based on a central thought, that one thought will be much more likely to impress the public mind than if the same series is based upon several *different* thoughts.

In a way, the whole system of trade-marks is built on this same basis. A trade-mark is desirable and necessary in order to give to the public mind a handle by which to grasp the name of a product. At the same time, this trade-mark becomes a mental receptacle in which the public mind can retain many of the good things which the different advertisements say about the product. In advertising a trade-mark, the aim is to impress it upon the average mind firmly, as if you stamped upon a compartment of the brain the name of that particular product. Thus the trade name becomes known, and, therefore, the product is more apt to be acceptable to the public. Then, to make that product more than acceptable, to make it *wanted*—to turn acceptability into demand—it is necessary to create a certain liking toward and favor for that name and the product for which it stands. In other words, it is necessary to build desire on top of familiarity with the name.

Just as it is necessary to concentrate on one audience with adequate space for a sufficient length of time in order to establish the trade-name with that audience, so it is even more necessary to pursue the same method when *persuading* the audience—when creating *desire* for the product.

We can fix a trade-name in the public mind more easily than some idea or ideas which will surround that trade-name with desire. If we wabble in our appeal, if this minute we talk to our audience in terms of the *utility* of the product, if the next we talk in terms of *beauty*, if the next minute we talk of *economy*, we are likely to miss our mark and fail to fix any one of these impressions. That is why it seems more effective to stick to one appeal, to pursue one angle of persuasion with sufficient continuity and repetition so that that angle may be finally forced into the mind and linked up as an element of desire in conjunction with the trade-name itself. On such continuity, on the repetition of a certain definite appeal or central idea, a campaign can well be bound together.

A central thought can be effective or ineffective, according to its piercing power: A generalized thought glances off the public mind; a concrete central thought *pierces*—providing it has the proper qualities to carry through. What are these qualities? They are those that almost any good sales message possesses, intensified in recognition of the fact that printed salesmanship lacks the personal force of a flesh-and-blood salesman and therefore must have an intrinsically greater strength. Some of these necessary qualities are:

1. *Interest:* The central thought must in itself have a definite concrete appeal which will attract; for instance, "A Skin You Love to Touch."
2. *Sincerity :* The central thought must be based on truth —truth which is sufficiently evident that it need not be proved by far-fetched tests. For instance. "Built Like a Sky-Scraper" is simple and sincere.
3. *Salesmanship:* It must be based on an appeal which is based on the *public's* interest rather than the self-

A contrast in looks. The twenty-year-ago page at upper right suggests cheapness. The modern "ad" below suggests taste.

Even though no candy is shown, there is something about this that makes one's mouth almost water. Henry C. Pragoff of the Lowney Advertising Department, calls this "one of the best of our advertisements. It proved mighty successful."

interest of the manufacturer. For instance, "You may dent the wood, but the varnish won't crack," instead of ".The largest varnish makers in the world."

To get this element of salesmanship into your central thought, it is usually best to find out from the consumers themselves just what point has the strongest appeal to them. This investigation should be made either by interviewing the ultimate purchasers with a set of questions, or by watching how goods of the same kind are actually bought over the counter.

Sometimes the central thought may become a fundamental of the advertising appeal—a fundamental so solid that it may be retained forever as the basis of the advertising appeal. In that event, it is best to interpret the fundamental central thought from different angles. For instance, the fundamental appeal may be some concrete idea in connection with "forging ahead in business." This fundamental appeal may be continuous, with its advertising angle varied by sometimes aiming it at the susceptibility of *fear*, sometimes *pride*, sometimes *luxury*, sometimes *love-of-power*.

The central thought should be utilized in the most complete possible way, not merely in the publication advertisements. It should also run through the booklets, or circulars, and even the packages, and it should permeate the personal salesmanship of the men on the road.

Of course, the central thought should not be tricky. It should not be obtrusive; it should be sufficiently indirect so that its "works" should not show on the surface. As to how long it should be continued, depends upon many considerations, but in general it is well to check up at the end of each six months and find out whether its repetition has approached tiresome monotony. In checking up, however, it is vital that the judgment be based upon the effect of the central thought upon the public mind, and *not* upon the advertiser's mind. The advertiser sees one advertisement one hundred times. He looks at it studiously and thoroughly; but the public gives an advertisement merely a glance. Therefore,

CONTINUITY THROUGH A CENTRAL THOUGHT 185

the advertiser is likely to tire of the central thought long before it becomes monotonous to the average prospect.

A slogan is not necessarily a central thought, although a central thought may become a slogan. A slogan may be a wonderful asset, or it may be no asset at all. The advertiser is likely to tire of the slogan prematurely, just as he is likely to tire of a central thought, forgetting that the public may have just come to the point of receiving the effect of that slogan. Like the central thought, which it helps to express, the slogan should be distinctive—it should be concrete, it should possess "you," it should be natural; it should not be tricky, or clever to the point of calling attention to itself. Like the central thought, the best slogans are chosen after long and thorough investigation of the consumer's point of view.

A new advertiser may find it best at first not to adopt a central thought, for the reason that an introduction and a favorable attention are quite as necessary in printed salesmanship as in personal salesmanship. It may therefore be best at first to meet the task of establishing prestige for the name of the advertiser and a general acceptance of his institution. The next step should probably be toward a plan of campaign which would tend to sell the advertiser's line on a merchandising basis. Then the plan may so evolve as to concentrate on a certain specialty, or specialties, with the appeal based upon a central thought. This central thought will probably build itself out of the results which the preliminary-prestige advertising establishes. Such a central thought can then fall on the fertile field of general good-will which the preparatory campaigns will have tilled.

Continuity, whether it be with or without a central thought, can be achieved through one or more of the following mechanical methods which are based on "eye-display," as described in Chapter VII:

1. *Trade-mark.* An example of this is the Victor Dog, in advertising Victrolas. It is interesting to note that an animal of this kind has an especial strength in

foreign countries. In fact, the Victrola, in foreign sales work, is called "His Master's Voice Gramophone."

2. *Trade 'characters.* Examples of this method of continuity are the Eskimo in Cliquot Club Ginger Ale, the cook in Cream of Wheat, and Aunt Jemima herself.

3. *Style of illustration.* For instance, the use of silhouettes in the Ricoro cigar campaign, the use of smart cartoons in Kelly-Springfield tire advertising, the use of dainty pastel tints in color, or the similar dainty voguish treatment, even in the black-and-white of Lux illustrations.

These mechanical methods of continuity are not in themselves central thoughts, although they may be accessory to the kind of continuity that is built around a real central thought. There are, at least, two other ways of achieving continuity by "mind-display" rather than "eye-display." Two of these methods are:

1. *Copy style.* One example is the style of copy which Irving Fletcher has written for Tecla Pearls. Another example is the phraseology of the Prince Albert tobacco advertisements.

2. *Slogans,* such as "Eventually, Why Not Now?" "It Beats as It Sweeps as It Cleans," "Ask the Man Who Owns One."

The best kind of continuity to strive for is the kind which possesses some or all of these mechanical "eye-display" methods, and either one of the two "mind-display" methods, plus a sensible, natural, interesting, persuasive sales-point, which is a real central thought, worthy of the hammer, hammer, hammer of repeated emphasis, on a fundamental, with such refreshing variations as time may require.

CHAPTER XXVI

Factors in the Selection of Media

After the detailed analysis of product and prospect, after the selection of plan of distribution, after the organization and inspiration of the sales force, there comes the question: "What is the best medium by which to carry my message to my prospective customers?" Media are too often selected first. This "cart-before-the-horse" error has caused many false starts in advertising campaigns; for the analysis of product, prospect, and distribution plans must help decide the question of "What media?"

For instance, it would be impossible to sell a mail-order house's product through street-car cards. Such selling usually requires the thorough persuasion of the person reading the advertisement. At least it requires more than mere suggestion. To get people to decide to send money for something, you must convince them that it is either cheaper or better than they could get elsewhere. The street-car card, with its limitations, would hardly be the place for a mail-order message. And so the very method of distribution may decide what medium should be used in advertising.

Every kind of medium has its advantages. A man with an open mind is often persuaded toward one medium, then the other, until he has almost come to believe that each one is the better. But the question of copy will help to determine what medium to use, just as the choice of medium will decide what kind of copy to use. For instance, if you decide to use street-car cards, you must use copy which is terse and simply suggestive; but you will have the advantage of colors with their excellent display value. If you choose magazines you will be able to use a beautiful half-tone of photographic effect, and you will have sufficient space to tell your story at some length, if you wish. If you choose the newspaper, you usually have to limit yourself to a certain kind of a line cut or zinc etching, and a brief statement; but you can take advantage of every element of timeliness in the relation of your product to current events. You need not make the mistake of a tailoring concern which tried to make use of this element in a national magazine which closes its forms many weeks in advance of issue. They came out in the fall with a $5,000 "ad" which showed Manager McGraw dressed in a suit of their make, and announced him as a principal in the World's Series, whereas during the month previous the Boston Braves had won the pennant, and Manager Stallings was the victor. If they had used newspapers, they could have changed their copy the night before.

Your method of distribution will not only help decide what kind of medium to use, but also will help decide what kind of copy. All these points, in turn, depend on the general analysis of product and of prospect. In other words, you must first pick to pieces the main elements of appeal that the product itself possesses and the main elements of the prospect's susceptibilities to which those points of appeal can best be directed. Then, almost automatically, the question of media will decide itself.

But a good deal of consumer advertising is done mainly to influence the dealer. The dealer will not be impressed unless the medium used is deemed by him to be powerful beyond question. The value of space always adds glamour. If the page cost is $5,000 it means more to the dealer than if it costs only $1,000. If he reads a certain medium, or if his wife reads it, he is more impressed for that reason. Some magazines recognize these facts and make a special effort to get dealer-subscribers—or to "merchandise" their medium to the dealers. In other words, they seek to persuade the dealer of the greatness of their publication as an advertising medium.

A practical factor in the selection of media is the kind of representatives the publications employ. The class of men who sell magazine space are notable for their ability to carry

This page at left was published in 1900; the one at right in 1920. Few trade-marks have undergone so little change. During that time, the Prudential has been almost alone in its field as a consistent advertiser.

This illustrates the value of close-ups. How much more interesting are these two persons whom you can really see, than the mass of thousands of people in the picture of twenty years ago.

a constructive story to the advertisers. Newspaper solicitors are more likely to devote themselves to mere details of contract, position, and price. Magazine representatives actually create business. As a result the magazines are sold better than any other media. Most new national advertisers are started by magazine men, who thus create business for their media.

A powerful solicitation is also exerted in favor of advertising novelties. This medium covers a wide field. Novelties are usually high in cost in comparison to number of persons reached, although they are theoretically low in cost per number of impressions made on each person. They can be made, however, to fit the thing advertised, and they permit of the use of colors; but, like street-car cards and outdoor signs, novelties are limited as to the message they can carry. They require abbreviation of the sales story. None of them can present your proposition as a salesman can. They simply remind and suggest.

As a rule, all such suggestive media are good for only such things as are already known and are wanted. A soda-cracker is wanted and is known. You need not tell people what soda-crackers are, and why they should want them. Your task would be to divert the demand for soda-crackers in general, to your soda-crackers in particular. The burden of your message is the name of your brand. Among such products there is usually sharp competition, for there are many manufacturers of every necessity. Such products are about on a par in regard to value: they are all of good quality; they all sell at about the same price. For any one of them, therefore, it is difficult to build up an advertising argument on the basis of price, or even quality.

But if you sell something that requires a thorough presentation—for instance, a cash register—you cannot make people buy by saying "cash register" to them over and over again. You have to convince your prospects of the reasons why they should consider the purchase of such a product. This requires persuasion. Such advertising cannot be put on a painted bulletin, or a street-car card, or an advertising novelty.

FACTORS IN THE SELECTION OF MEDIA 191

Any one of these media may be used to supplement an educational campaign which is built on persuasion; but alone it could hardly carry the load, simply because people read such media "on the run." Thus, the character of your message helps determine the media. If you have a long story to tell you must get your audience "seated." If you just want to drop them a hint, you may deliver it "on the run," with good success.

Another factor in the choice of media is the amount you can spend in advertising. If you have a small appropriation, so that an extensive general campaign is out of the question, you will have to select media which will make it possible for you to start a campaign without risking a large amount of money at once. If you limit your campaign to a certain community, and you spend $1,000 to the result of $100 worth of profit for that unit of your market, you can later duplicate that same campaign in almost every other city in the country.

Of course you cannot be sure from just one experiment whether or not the same advertising will succeed to the same degree throughout the nation, but if you try it out in three or four different localities, with the same success, you will know that you can afford to spend enough to cover the United States; and the great advantage of this system is that you can work step by step. You can take the income from one territory and invest it in another.

Usually a new product is launched with very little capital. Very often the promoter must borrow deeply to undertake any advertising campaign at all. But even then he cannot get enough to buy very much space in the general publications and thus cover the country quickly. Perhaps even his unit experiments will fail at first. He may find he has not hit upon the right formula. Either the copy is wrong or he is using too large space or too little space, or he has not established the proper relations with the trade. But by this kind of experimentation he can find the cause of his failure, and knowing the cause, he can change the method accordingly.

At first an advertising appropriation has to be greater than the increased profits will justify. But on an established business the amount to be spent on advertising is usually based on some percentage of the expected sales. This percentage varies according to the amount of money necessary, and according to the size of the possible profit. Here is a statement of the average percentage of advertising appropriations in 13 different lines of business:

	Percentage of Gross Sales
Beverages	10%
Mail-order	10%
Cleansing powders	10%
Smoking tobacco	6%
Auto accessories	5¼%
Cigarettes	5%
Phonographs	5%
Paint	3½%
Shirts	3½%
Office furniture	3%
Cameras	3%
Soap	3%

Of course there are many big users of local media who also use national publications. They cannot tell which class of media is best and they can afford to duplicate their advertising effort. But on some other articles the margin is so small, or the field so limited, that it is necessary to keep the advertising down to the barest minimum, and to select the one best medium rather than to use several whose fields more or less overlap each other.

The extent of territory in which the advertiser can sell will help him to decide the question of media; at least, this consideration will exclude certain media, because if your field of selling is limited you will naturally not want to advertise in media which extend beyond it, for you would then pay for the entire circulation, when only part of it could possibly do you any good. So important is this point that some large publications—particularly in the agricultural field—divide their issues into two editions, eastern and western. The advertiser can then circulate his "ad" in whichever half of the nation he can best cover. The editorial contents are the same in both.

FACTORS IN THE SELECTION OF MEDIA

The following estimate shows the trend in the selection of media:

Medium	Total Annual Advertising Expenditures	
	1916	1919
Newspapers	$380,000,000	$490,000,000
Magazines	65,000,000	150,000,000
Business papers	40,000,000	125,000,000
Street-cars	5,000,000	5,000,000
Signs and novelties	75,000,000	70,000,000
Direct mail, etc.	175,000,000	300,000,000
	$740,000,000	$1,140,000,000

CHAPTER XXVII

The Daily Newspaper as a Medium

Four hundred and ninety million dollars, according to reliable estimates, are annually spent in newspaper advertising. Of this national advertisers spend about $155,000,000, local advertisers $335,000,000. In the United States there are over 10,000 towns, each of which boasts one or more newspapers. Foremost are the English-language daily newspapers. Of these there are 2,100 with a combined circulation of 28,000,-000. Then there are about 15,000 weeklies of two distinct kinds: Those which are known as "home print" papers, which are completely printed in the shop of the local publisher, and are, therefore, more likely to have a thoroughly local flavor; and the semi-home, or "patent inside" papers which come to the local publisher with one side already printed, the other side to be run off on the publisher's own press. By using that "patent inside," the publisher saves money by escaping a large part of the cost of setting up his own type for those two inside pages, and printing the entire paper himself. The syndicate which supplies him with "patent insides," prints many thousands of these papers, with the two inside pages all the same. Some 5,000 publishers get their half-printed paper in the same way and print the local news on the two outside pages.

The usual cost of newspaper space is less than one-fifth of a cent per line per thousand of circulation. The cost becomes about one seventh of a cent per line per thousand for the big newspapers where the circulation runs up to 100,000. But the smaller newspaper cannot afford to sell its space at so low a rate. The usual paper of 1,000 circulation has to charge about 20 cents per inch per thousand.

In the use of small newspapers individually to cover the country, an expensive detail is that of sending out thousands of insert orders and electros separately, and checking them, and paying the bills. You would have to pay each paper every month. This might mean that you would have several hundred bills a day to pay. But by using 5,000 ready-print papers you can order the syndicate press to include your ad on the pages which they print in advance. In that case only one order, two electros, and one bill are necessary.

Of course, any advertiser would prefer to have his "ad" where the live local matter is—on the home-print pages. But the syndicate is able so to reduce the cost of production of the ready prints that the cost for space on its "inside" pages is below that in the local pages. Indeed, so economical are ready prints that in hundreds of cases the ready-print price for a given thousand will be 3 cents an inch as against a price of 10 cents an inch on the local page.

As a local medium there is nothing better than the newspaper. It reaches just the people the local advertiser can reach and wants to reach. Its economy is not so important to the local advertiser because, as a rule, he finds it necessary and profitable to use the local newspaper, even though it is considerably higher in price. So natural is it for the newspaper to count on the local or home advertising as its main advertising, that when the publishers first began to accept contracts for space from outsiders they called them "Foreign" advertising. The rate at first was high and decidedly in favor of the local advertiser. To-day this differential is practically eliminated; in the cases of many of the larger newspapers wholly so.

Rates for department-store advertising are usually especially low; this is the largest class of newspaper advertising, as the table on next page, covering six months in a typical metropolitan newspaper, indicates.

Newspaper rates usually vary with the amount of space used. A maximum rate is charged when minimum space is used, and vice versa. Some papers reduce their charges according to the frequency of insertion. In these cases, one inch every day during the year will earn a far lower rate than 365 inches all at one time. Such a system of rates is called

Class	Lines Used	Percentage
Amusements	121,189	1.7%
Automobiles	447,933	6%
Department Stores	2,139,540	30%
Financial	134,215	1.9%
Food	331,393	5%
Furniture	460,917	6.5%
Hotels, Resorts, and Restaurants	9,313	.00132%
Instruction	18,274	.0026%
Jewelry and Silverware	50,012	.0071%
Beverages	6,313	.0009%
Legal and Public Notices	33,310	.00475%
Musical Instruments	155,936	2.22%
Publishers	36,026	.005%
Proprietary Medical and Toilet Articles	459,640	6.5%
Railroads and Steamships	31,350	.0044%
Real Estate	563,233	8%
Shoes	238,923	3%
Tobacco	102,071	1.4%
Wants	797,322	11%
Miscellaneous	875,050	12%
Total	7,011,960	

Table showing amount of different classes of advertising in typical city paper for six months.

a "fixed-space" basis. The "open-space" plan does not take into consideration the frequency of insertion so much as it does the total amount of space used during a certain period.

Other considerations also decide the cost of newspaper space. If you do not furnish your advertisement in plate form, and the newspapers, therefore, have to set up your "ad," you may have to pay a composition charge of 5 cents per inch or more to cover the cost of the labor involved. The usual big city newspapers do not make this charge. You need only send them "copy," not electrotypes, of the "ad" already set up. They will be quite sure to follow the style you indicate. But most of the smaller papers cannot do the composition work without extra charge, nor can you expect them to set up your "ads" in any special way. They have few varieties of type, and probably not the one you want.

The usual advertising rate is based on "run-of-paper"

position, which means that the publisher has a right to insert the "ad" anywhere he desires. If a special, or "preferred," position is specified, an extra charge is usually stipulated. Here are the different positions and extra charges for each, from the rate-card of a typical newspaper:

Name of Position	What It Means	Extra Charge Per Line
Next to reading.	Advertisement to be inserted with reading matter alongside it.	.10
Top of column.	Advertisement to be inserted at top of column.	.20
Under and next reading.	Advertisement to be inserted immediately under, and alongside reading matter.	.20
Top of column and next reading.	Advertisement to be inserted at top of column, surrounded on three sides by reading matter.	.40

Extra charge is sometimes exacted for position on special pages, such as society, editorial, etc.

The newspaper offers the advantage of linking up the position of an "ad" with the element of timeliness, for it is possible to place your "ad" where the character of continuous matter will strengthen the force of its message. A millinery announcement, for instance, may be most effective on a society page. Haberdashery sales are often advertised on the sporting page. You can also make your announcement correspond, to a day, with a particular event. You can fit your "ad" to the occasion. If it appears the day before the Fourth of July, you can surround it with the atmosphere of the Fourth, and thus make it more effective.

Another big advantage of newspaper advertising is that it enables you to check up the results. You can tell whether or not your expenditure in a certain town is justified. Suppose you are using a thousand inches a year in a certain paper as your advertising appropriation for that city. You can tell from your books how much business you are getting out of that city. If it is not enough to justify the expenditure, you know that your advertising in this locality is not successful. This may be due to your choice of medium, or to your copy. It may be because you have the wrong local representation, or because your advertising has not run long enough, or a competitor's advertising is stronger. It may be due to any one or to several causes.

If you were using general publications and the proportion of your advertising expense for that city was $2,000, then you could not tell whether that certain part of your advertising was profitable. Sometimes the same advertising in one locality will yield good profit, and in another locality will incur a loss. And so, the ability to check up each city in this way is perhaps the greatest advantage that newspaper advertising offers the men who seek a national market.

A disadvantage of the newspaper is its brevity of life. It is read to-day and thrown away to-morrow at the latest, while the magazine is kept. If, however, the effect of advertising is mainly, if not wholly, in the first impression it makes, then the advertisement which is seen many times does not possess much more power to persuade than that which is seen once or twice—for, that which we see again and again we do not notice. Perhaps, then, the fact of the short life of a newspaper "ad" is not, after all, so great an objection.

Another element is that of atmosphere. The magazine is not only of a comparatively high grade artistically, but it contains a better quality of matter. This extends even to advertising pages: magazines often refuse to accept medical advertising, even when it is of proved merit—a point often emphasized in favor of this medium—because an "ad" is supposed to be flavored by the company it keeps. If, for instance, an automobile "ad" is surrounded by medical advertisements, its effectiveness is less than it would be if it were surrounded by advertisements of silks and clothing.

Then, too, there are certain mechanical limitations to the newspaper. It has to be printed on cheap print paper which cannot reproduce a very good half-tone. The illustration in the newspapers must either be a line cut made from zinc or wood, or else it must be a very coarse-screen half-tone, which cannot possibly show up as photographically as a finer-screen on smoother paper. In fact, the main objection to advertising in the newspapers is this matter of illustration. You cannot present as dainty or as forceful an appeal as you can when smooth paper and fine-screened half-tones make possible the perfect reproduction of the finest art.

CHAPTER XXVIII

Sunday Newspapers and Newspaper Co-operation

The huge size of the usual Sunday newspaper has been regarded as a disadvantage to advertisers on the ground that an advertisement in such an edition would have to compete against too many other features as well as advertisements. This disadvantage, however, is somewhat overcome by the fact that the reader has more leisure to apply to a Sunday newspaper than to a daily newspaper. Especially is this true of the women. Men usually find time to cover their daily newspapers rather thoroughly, but some women devote as much time to the Sunday newspaper as to all the other editions of the week.

That is one reason why the Sunday newspaper is more and more favorably regarded as a medium by which to reach women. The consensus of opinion is that 80% of all retail buying is done by women. There are many actual examples that indicate that this is the fact—for instance, a perfumer appealing to women found that $6,000 worth of advertising in a Sunday newspaper brought in 31,000 orders for samples at 10 cents apiece.

The Sunday newspaper is a group of several different publications: one section is devoted to general news, another to editorials, one to automobiles, another to real estate, another to sports; and there is usually a rotogravure section, or a magazine section of some kind. It is important to decide in which section you wish your advertisement to appear.

The rotogravure section of a Sunday newspaper is regarded with growing favor, because of its proved results, and because it is logically the preferred section of a newspaper. The rotogravure approaches most nearly to actual photographic reproduction—that fact is responsible for its popularity.

In 1920 there were only 48 different newspapers with rotogravure sections, although these papers totalled a circulation of 5,500,000 readers. Full-page units have been the popular size for advertising in rotogravure, and it is usually best for an advertiser to use not less than ¼ page. The reason for this is simply that to take full advantage of the virtue of rotogravure it is necessary to use pictures, and to use them in a fairly close-up manner. Then, too, rotogravure has a certain disadvantage in that it cannot reproduce type matter as sharply as can black-and-white mediums. For this reason it is necessary to use larger type, and therefore larger space.

The price of rotogravure advertising is considerably greater than the straight black-and-white advertising, but about the same as the cost of the majority of magazines, circulation and general quality considered. However, the cost of plate work is saved in using rotogravure, because the advertiser has only to furnish to the newspaper a photograph of the illustration and type proof of the text material. From this material the advertisement is reproduced in the rotogravure.

A virtue of Sunday and daily newspapers is the assistance which they render to the advertiser in:

(a) Readvertising the consumer advertising to the trade.

(b) Assisting the manufacturer's sales force, should the territory be unfamiliar to the salesman or crew.

This newspaper co-operation takes many forms, and is usually of particular value to the manufacturer who is entering the territory for the first time as an advertiser, and whose products need wide-spread distribution. Some newspapers prepare a complete analysis of the local marketing conditions for each particular class of merchandise. Their investigators interview large buyers, determine the strength of competition, the possibilities for success for the prospective advertiser, and submit recommendations as to how the market may best be approached. Other newspapers prepare complete route lists of the dealers in their city, with street maps showing location of the various classes of dealers. In addition to the dealer's name, credit ratings are frequently given, as well as other data concerning the dealer and his store.

Some newspapers prepare elaborate portfolios for the use of salesmen, showing reprints of the advertising to be used in the newspaper, and containing for the salesman a general letter of introduction from the publisher to the trade. In other cases newspapers advertise the manufacturer's advertising to the trade by direct mail, usually just as the sales work starts, if distribution for the product is required—or at the start of the advertising campaign, if the product has already sufficient distribution. This mail work frequently takes the form of elaborate broadsides, which are mailed to present dealers and prospective dealers. Such broadsides show reprints of advertising to be used, schedule of insertions, data concerning window displays and dealer helps available from the manufacturer, information regarding "free deals" and introductory sales offers, if any. These go out over the signature of the newspaper. Perhaps a return post-card, requesting window-and-store-advertising material, or requesting a salesman to call, will be mailed with broadsides or letters. Sometimes a proof, or proofs, of some of the advertisements are mailed to the trade, with a letter from the newspaper telling the dealer about the campaign and urging him to co-operate. In cases where full pages are used proofs of the copy are mailed to the trade so that the store receives the proof the same day the advertisement appears. The dealer is urged to paste the proof upon his door or window at once, to identify his store with the newspaper advertising.

Frequently window-display contests for a manufacturer's product are arranged by the newspapers. Cash prizes for best displays are offered to dealers. The newspaper secures entrants, arranges for judging the displays, awards the prizes, and handles all details. Other newspapers confine their co-operation to the publication of a separate newspaper, written especially for retail stores of all classes. This is their medium for keeping in touch with the trade. Through this the newspaper announces coming advertising campaigns, suggests, store arrangement, dealer's advertising plans, details of "what

SUNDAY NEWSPAPERS AND CO-OPERATION

the other fellow is doing," etc. Some trade publications, such as these, are quite elaborate and exert a tremendous influence on the trade in behalf of the advertiser's product.

Most newspapers extend co-operation on a definite amount of space to be used during the campaign, *i. e.*, 5,000, 10,000, or 20,000 agate lines of space to be used within the year. Some newspapers desire a non-cancellable contract, so that they may count on the promises which they may make to dealers regarding the campaign. The amount of space required to warrant newspaper co-operation is usually determined by the newspaper, based upon its knowledge and experience of the size of campaign required in its territory to insure an "over-the-counter" movement of the product for the dealer.

About 100 newspapers are thoroughly organized with a separate department to give co-operation. But there is no standard of service, as shown by the following answers to a questionnaire sent to 200 papers:

73% of the newspapers mail broadsides or letters to the trade for national advertisers.

27% refused to mail either broadside or letters.

66% of the newspapers that mail broadsides or letters charge postage to the advertisers.

29% of the newspapers that mail broadsides or letters make a charge for stuffing, sealing, and stamping.

14% of the newspapers will sell products to retailers for manufacturers who are advertising in their local columns.

86% refuse to sell goods.

81% of the newspapers will introduce salesmen to the trade.

(The great majority of these newspapers limit the introduction to jobbers and the leading retailers of their city.)

82% of the newspapers make a market survey upon request, while

18% refuse to give this service.

CHAPTER XXIX

Magazines, Class and Trade Publications

In the words of John M. Siddall, editor of *The American Magazine:*
"No engine equals the national magazine for making us all nearer alike and all better. It is the great potential standardizer of modern times. It is the messenger between distant localities—the carrier of the new idea that is valuable, and the stabilizer of the old idea that is worth while. It is just beginning to exercise its full powers. The faster we develop into one people, the greater will the magazine be, because it is founded on a simple big idea that is sound. The inhabitants of the United States are thinking more and more in national terms. It is better for them that they should think so. The magazines have fostered this idea—advertised it. They themselves will be the beneficiaries of the idea, as well as the promoters of it. A stronger and more closely connected country—articulating as one big body—will automatically bring stronger and greater magazines, because of the opportunity and the need. This is the direction in which the current has turned—and it will have its way. The world will not go back to changing cars eleven times on the road from New York to Chicago. Nor will it go back to the idea of the walled city. It has had a look beyond the horizon. It is interested in what it has seen—and wants to see more."

Magazines originally supported themselves on the subscriptions of their readers. Advertising was only incidental. To-day, few magazines can live on their subscriptions. Almost always the cost to secure a subscription is as much or more than the subscription amounts to. The advertising which the modern magazine carries is the backbone of the profit of the publication. The magazine-advertising expenditure in the United States now approaches $150,000,000 per year.

There are several different classes of magazines. The main group comprises the general magazines, of which there are about 150 in the United States. These, in turn, divide into weeklies, such as the *Saturday Evening Post*, and monthlies, such as *The American Magazine*. The monthlies, in turn, are divided into fiction magazines, such as the *Red Book*, and review magazines, such as *World's Work*. Then there is the mechanical division between those magazines which are large and are called "flat," and those magazines which are small, like *Scribner's* and the *Atlantic Monthly*, which are called "standard," because they are the shape and size and style of binding which have been standard for magazines for the last half-century.

Among the women's magazines there are about 50. Some of these are general, such as the *Ladies' Home Journal*, others have to do particularly with fashions, such as *McCall's*, with domestic science, such as *Good Housekeeping*, with motherhood, such as *Mothers' Magazine*, and embroidery, such as *Needlecraft Magazine*. In general, women's magazines have the most responsive circulation of any class of media. For that reason they are greatly favored for advertising purposes. Their cost, however, is slightly greater than the general magazine, circulation considered. For instance, the largest women's magazine costs two-thirds of a cent per line per thousand of circulation, whereas the largest general magazine costs one-half cent per line per thousand of circulation.

There are certain publications which are designed primarily for mail-order work, and although these are not generally known, their circulations are considerable. There are about 30 of these mail-order papers, including such periodicals as *Comfort*, with a circulation of over 1,000,000, *Household* of Kansas, with a circulation of 750,000, and *Home Life*, with a circulation almost as large. The readers of these papers are, as a rule, responsive to mail-order appeals, either because they have acquired the habit of ordering by mail, or because, living in out-of-the-way places, they can more easily buy by mail, or for some other reason. For general publicity, however, these media are not so effective, because they do not have the prestige which makes their use impressive to the trade.

In addition to the general magazines, the women's magazines, and the mail-order publications, there are nearly 1,000 religious publications. Then, too, there are over 500 agricultural publications, of which a few are national, such as *The Farm Journal*, with a circulation of over 1,000,000, and *Farm and Fireside*, and *The Country Gentleman*. Most farm papers, however, are either localized as to territory or specialized as to class. Of the localized media, most are confined within the limits of a State. As to the class agricultural publications, most are confined to some specialization, such as horse-breeding, dairying, fruit-growing, or poultry-raising.

In most cases each magazine has its own selling force, in which they differ from the custom in the newspaper field, where as many as 20 or more newspapers may all be represented by one organization. It is difficult for one corps of men to sell the advertising space for 20 or so newspapers. They cannot work effectively for any one newspaper, as can the salesman for a magazine, who can adequately give all the arguments in favor of his magazine as well as those in favor of magazine advertising in general.

The magazine is sold on the basis of the page as a unit, but, usually, you can buy as small a space as seven lines, or half an inch of one column. The cost is figured on the circulation. This figures out about three times as much as the same circulation per line in newspapers—an average of two-thirds of a cent per line per thousand of circulation. But when both the newspaper and magazine are figured on the basis of a page, the cost is found to be about the same per page per thousand of circulation in either medium. In other words, a magazine of 100,000 circulation may cost per page about $500. A newspaper with 100,000 circulation may cost about the same amount per page. But, of course, the newspaper page is several times the size of the usual magazine page.

One virtue of the magazine is that its readers are at leisure.

MAGAZINES, CLASS AND TRADE PUBLICATIONS 207

They tend to concentrate more on a magazine, whether reading matter or advertisements, than on a newspaper. Still, the competition against your magazine "ad" is keen, for all the other attractions in the magazines are competing for the reader's attention. A person is likely to be more deeply engrossed in a magazine article or story than in anything he sees in the newspaper. Consequently, you have a hard task to attract his eye toward your "ad" and away from the magazine's features.

If your "ads" in the magazine are scattered among the reading pages, they suffer the competition of adjacent reading matter. If they are all gathered in a group at the back of the magazine, they compete against each other—but not to the degree that street-car cards or outdoor signs do. Magazine "ads" engage considerable voluntary attention. They seem to be the one kind of paid displays that many seek and all seem to enjoy. They do not have to compel the eye with sheer display. Some magazine advertisements attract through the appeal of art. Others have a literary appeal. Others rely on a cartoon. Still others whisper enticingly in terms of daintiness. Few coerce attention through optical force. Magazine "ads" are more versatile than newspaper "ads," street-car cards, or signs. The eye can run over a hundred magazine "ads" and not get tired because they offer a refreshing variety. This is because of the magazine's superiority in printing as well as in the degree of voluntary attention which a magazine "ad" enjoys.

In its scope of circulation the general magazine is growing more and more like the newspaper. A magazine's readers are no longer of a distinctive class. At least, the large modern magazine is read by Tom, Dick, and Harry; Mary, Jane, and Maud. Except for certain "class periodicals," magazine circulation is the general public, just as newspaper circulation is.

The element of timeliness can be used only slightly in the magazine. There is no chance to take advantage of the weather, for instance. Most magazines go to press at least a month before their date of publication. Therefore, the only

208 A SHORT COURSE IN ADVERTISING

timeliness that can be approached is the matter of seasons and occasions of the calendar. Efforts to capitalize these even, are dangerous, because there are other "ads" in the same magazine (though they announce different things) that may also have capitalized the element of timeliness in the same way. All such "ads" will then be less effective because they thus compete in their line of appeal.

The magazine does not permit you to cut the cloth to fit your suit. You frequently have to pay for much waste circulation. If your distribution is not perfect you must pay to send your message to places where your goods are not on sale. This fault is less pronounced in class publications such as agricultural, motor-boat, automobile, gardening, and fashion periodicals, as well as many others whose circulations depend upon certain characteristics of their readers. Magazines of general circulation depend on common tastes possessed by all. Class publications presuppose distinctive interests and desires, and consequently their space costs more per inch per reader than space in general magazines. As a rule, such a publication is used only for those products which particularly appeal to its respective class.

Certain specialized papers are called trade journals, or business papers, if they pertain to furniture, grain, or some other specific phase of business. If their editorial policy is professional or scientific, they are called technical publications. But each of these has the common trait of such publications —its circulation comprises a clientele of tastes peculiar to a certain class.

There are over 3,000 of these class and trade publications. Almost every line of business has one or more—some national and some local. For instance, advertising has 20; architecture and building have about 75; dry-goods trade, 15; banking, 90; medical, nearly 200; hospitals, 15. Even to dogs and cats as many publications are devoted as to the hardware business, and 38 trade papers are devoted to cows. Chickens, however, have over 60 publications, whereas nuts have only 5.

CHAPTER XXX

Street-Car, Theatre, and Outdoor Media

Just as you can use the newspaper in a localized way, so you can use the street-car card, the theatre program, theatre-curtain, the moving-picture, the stereopticon slide, the painted bulletin, and the outdoor poster. With all these, except the theatre program the theoretical cost per thousand of circulation is exceptionally low. The theatre program is in many respects a class medium. All of these mediums are usually used supplementally—as a reinforcement to publication advertising.

The fact that full colors can be used is a strong argument in favor of street-car cards. This point is particularly important in connection with the advertisement of packaged goods, where the aim is mainly to familiarize the public with the article and the trade-mark. Here colors make possible the reproduction of the package in actual size, and impress the article on the person's mind far more intensely than could any number of words. The timeliness of the street-car-card impression is another argument. As a rule, the shopper sees the street-car card while on the way to buy. Consequently, the street-car "ad" may have the last word in the persuasion of that shopper as to what particular brand to buy. Of course, this same argument holds just as true as to the cards and signs that a manufacturer has in the dealer's store.

Each street-car card must face tremendous competition. Its whole environment is advertising—on all sides. Car cards enjoy little voluntary interest, such as advertisements may receive in a newspaper or the magazine for which the reader has paid. Only involuntary interest does the street-car card enjoy.

In their competition with each other, street-car cards use all sorts of colors to win the attention of the casual eye. This tends to create confusion. The result is a tendency to flood the specific message of a certain card with a conglomeration of all the cards. Experiments have been made to ascertain how far this fusion does blur the reader's consciousness. For instance, in one city the ice-cream makers did considerable advertising in street-cars. In glancing over the ads of three different ice-creams, nine out of ten could not recall which "ad" belonged to which ice-cream company. The copy of each was extremely individual. But in running over those street-car cards, the eye was pulled this way and that, so much so that the comprehension was really blurred.

Street-car space is sold at the rate of about 50 cents per card per month, and usually on a six or twelve month contract. The standard street-car size is 11 x 21 inches. The advertiser must furnish his own cards, which cost from $40 to $100 per thousand, according to the quantity and the design. In addition to full-runs, which means one card in every car in the territory covered—half-runs are sold, calling for a card in each alternate car. A slightly higher price prevails for half-runs or quarter-runs.

Almost every complete advertising program has in it stereopticon slides, because when they are used they are so effective, and because it costs so little to furnish slides. Usually the dealer pays for having these slides shown in his local moving-picture theatre, and therefore the expense to the advertiser is only 40 or 50 cents, representing merely the cost of the slide. In the usual picture-house only a few slides are used during each performance and, as a result, each is quite effective. The main objections to a stereopticon slide are that you cannot control their use and that you intrude on the public attention at a time when it seeks entertainment for which it has paid. Your message is, therefore, in danger of being received with a resentment which may hurt your good-will.

Of course the moving-picture has become an important advertising medium, although it still offers a great many obstacles against its effective use. The cost of producing a moving-picture for advertising purposes is not so prohibitive

These miniature reproductions of a series of car cards show how continuity can be carried through a campaign.

All the cards are alike in their main general elements, but in the originals there is a refreshing variation of color, in addition to the variation of subject, which so happily averts monotony. One of the great virtues of car cards is their ability to show food products in actual size and natural colors.

—from $1.00 per foot to $5.00 per foot, depending on conditions, for the cost of the original, or "negative." Duplicates, or "positives," can be secured at from 10 cents or 20 cents per foot. The big difficulty comes after you have your picture. If it has enough selling value to justify your advertising investment, you will find it very hard to get it into good moving-picture theatres. Almost every one of the country's 15,000 moving-picture exhibitors is jealous of the good-will of his audience, and is afraid to jeopardize that good-will by intruding a moving-picture with a commercial hook to it, no matter how interesting that picture may be.

In certain cities agencies have been formed to take over the circulation of advertising moving-pictures, and, except in cases of the largest and best houses, these agencies have been rather successful in getting the exhibitor to accept money for allowing the advertising picture to be projected in his theatre. The usual cost to the advertiser for this privilege in the average theatre is $2.00 to $4.00 a performance.

There are two other mediums through which to advertise to theatre audiences—one is the theatre program and the other is the theatre-curtain. In a few cases the theatre program distributed around a number of different theatres, with the advertisements remaining standard in each separate program. In New York City you can buy full-page space in a program circulated in 52 theatres at a total cost of $22,000 per page per year, with an annual circulation of 14,000,000. In some playhouses there are usually four or five advertisements on the theatre-curtain, each occupying a space about 4x3 feet. As a rule, these spaces are exclusive—only one advertiser in each line is allowed a place on the curtain. The average price for an advertisement of this kind is usually $4.00 or $5.00 per week.

Outdoor media are divided into three general classes: Posters, painted bulletins, and electric signs. The posters or bill-boards are sold either locally by the owners, or nationally by an authorized company representing them. Billboards are of standard height—nine feet. The usual unit is a "sheet" 28x42 inches. Most posters are 24 sheets—four sheets high by six wide. The cost is from $7 to $10 a month for the posting and showing of each 24-sheet poster. The paper costs extra—from $1.00 to $2.00 per board. The names of local dealers can be imprinted on each poster. Special locations and illuminated boards cost from $15 to $50 or more per month per showing. Poster locations cannot be selected by the advertiser. He arbitrarily is given certain boards, depending on whether he buys a full-showing, a double-showing, or a half-showing. A full-showing usually means about

STREET-CAR, THEATRE, AND OUTDOOR MEDIA   213

SOME 24-SHEET POSTERS

The Peace Treaty Poster was all prepared in advance. The minute the signing was cabled, wires went out to almost every poster plant in the country. In some cases they were on the boards before the "extras" were on the street.

one poster to each one thousand of population. Three-sheet posters cost from $2.00 to $5.00 per month, exclusive of the necessary lithographed paper for posting.

Painted bulletins are "ads" that are painted directly on the sign-boards. They are, therefore, not so suited to change as are the paper posters which are pasted on. Except for that, the painted bulletin and the poster are about the same. The price, however, is about twice as great as for posters.

This price includes painting—usually twice or three times a year. Painted walls cost less than painted bulletins, size considered. Electric signs are usually localized. Some manufacturers, however, seek to cover the country, and offer to furnish such signs for national advertisers in a country-wide way. Rates differ according to size and location. Some cost as high as from $20,000 to $30,000 and more per year.

The fewer painted bulletins, electric signs, and posters, the more effective they are. For instance, if the whole side of a big building is covered with signs, no matter how wonderful in color or size your sign may be, it is worth comparatively little, because the adjoining signs so hammer at the eye of the passer-by that he cannot get any particular kind of an impression. But if your sign is there alone it is worth many, many times more in its ability to flash its message to those who see it.

The main thing that differentiates the electric sign from every other sign, with the exception of the mechanical window display, is the feature of action. Action has a greater eye-attraction than color. On this point there is nothing like the electric sign. Electric signs make possible the use of both color and action. Also, they are usually located so that they reach people where they can buy the thing advertised.

With signs you can select your territory. For instance, if a miller seeks to sell rye flour for the housewife to make her own bread, he will find that the best market for that kind of flour is in a certain kind of district. With a sign, he can reach right into that section and concentrate every cent of his appropriation on that immediate market.

Very little copy should go on a poster or a car card. S. A. Riebel, advertising manager of Yuban Coffee, expresses this principle as follows:

"In my opinion, the most valuable car-card from an impressionistic standpoint is where the two separate and distinct impressions—the color scheme through the eye, and the message (the thought) through the mind—both flash the brain at the same time, and tell the same story.

"Car-card advertising is much like poster and bulletin

advertising in that it is read by most people at a glance—in a flash. When your color scheme attracts, the flash or message should tell the story, and this story, to be read quickly, must of necessity be brief—but it must also tell the whole story and be just brimful of human appeal."

CHAPTER XXXI

Demonstrating, Sampling, and Sales Aids

In the twilight zone between advertising and selling come the important items of sampling and demonstrating. And sampling and demonstrating, in turn, frequently merge into each other. Sampling has usually been regarded as giving something for nothing. But, in the modern sense, sampling is, in most cases, selling at a very low price a trial size of a product. The tendency away from free samples is due to the growing conviction that a free sample cheapens the public appreciation of a product; and for that reason discourages repeat purchase on the part of the consumer. Then, too, the offer of free samples in advertising has frequently led to inquiries from people who were not interested and who were not possible purchasers. Indiscriminate distribution is also subject to wasteful throwing away of samples, or selling at small price on the part of the sampler.

To make sampling an adjunct to advertising, some advertisers ask the reader to write for a sample, so that she may find out for herself just how good the product is. The results of such action-getting advertising are more easily traced than in general publicity. If $500 in a certain national medium will bring only 500 requests for a 10-cent sample of your goods, and if $500 in another magazine of the same circulation brings 1,600 inquiries, then you can see that the latter is better for the advertising of that product.

Still another way to key results is to use the advertising as a means to distribute literature. Many large advertisers use this system. They announce a booklet to be had on request. By this plan the advertisement itself tells enough of the story so as to make the reader say: "Well, that sounds like a pretty good thing—I'd like to know more about it." With interest thus created, the fuller explanation which the booklet makes possible may create an active desire in the reader and thus cause a sale. As to the value of the plan of offering a booklet in periodical advertising, one big concern tried an interesting experiment. Six "ads" which did not feature a booklet produced a total of but 231 inquiries and 57 sales. Two "ads" only, which featured a book, produced 644 inquiries and 434 sales.

To "key" an "ad" means to tag it with a sign of some sort so that you can tell which magazine produced each inquiry. In one magazine you may specify that the request should be sent to a certain address, and in each other magazine you may specify a different address. This different address, or different "department number," is the key by which the advertiser can tell from which publication the inquiry came. For getting inquiries, the coupon is a favorable method. About twenty years ago the coupon was a new idea. Advertisers found it was a general success. But so many have used it that people have more or less got accustomed to seeing coupons and their effectiveness has waned. Still, the coupon has elements which frequently make it worth the space it takes. The coupon suggests to the mind the idea to inquire for further information. It appeals to the laziness of the prospect because it saves the trouble of getting a piece of stationery on which to write the inquiry. These two factors have made the coupon successful in increasing the number of answers that an "ad" produces—as against what that same advertisement would bring without any coupon.

Inquiry-getting is a small by-product of the usual modern advertising campaign. In fact, the tendency is away from seeking answers to each advertisement. Many national advertisers have passed through a period of seeking inquiries, while they were trying out advertising, and wanted to convince themselves that people really saw advertisements. Presently they withdrew the offer of a booklet from their copy. Successively they usually pass through these stages:

a. Introducing their product to a few people and seeking to use inquiries in getting distribution.

b. Introducing it to more people and using inquiries on their dealers to encourage larger and more regular orders.
  c. Planting a subconscious knowledge of their product in the public's mind so that when a dealer shows it to the prospect it will strike a responsive note.
  d. Getting people to ask for their product when in need of such a product. In this stage the inquiry-seeking is usually dropped.
  e. Making the name of the brand better known than the article itself—just as Uneeda is better known than biscuit.

Another way to convert the influence of general advertising into concrete results is through out-and-out sampling—aggressive giving away of samples by personal house-to-house distribution, or sending samples to a selected list. This method is worked so thoroughly that in almost every town in the country there is an official distributer, whose business it is to deliver samples and booklets in that locality. The cost, exclusive of the cost of the samples, is around $4 per thousand samples.

A big coffee roaster found sampling the solution of one of his problems, in this way: He sold his coffee to the dealer at about 35 cents a pound. The dealer got 40 cents a pound for it, and it was advertised at that price. In order to get every dealer to stock up with his brand of coffee, this roaster had to have a particularly good argument as to why a dealer should be forced to take only a nickel a pound profit on his kind instead of the usual larger margin. His argument was that it was much easier for the grocer to sell his brand.

To make his argument true this roaster had a number of young women go out through each neighborhood and call at the homes in the dealer's locality. They explained about the coffee and asked for the privilege of going in and making a cup of coffee for the woman of the house. The coffee proved so good that the housewife would usually say: "You may enter my order for a pound." The demonstrators would gather these orders and then go to the grocery store and say: "Here are orders for fifty pounds, and of these fifty people I guess there are about forty of them to whom you do not sell. Possibly about thirty buy their coffee from some mail-order house, or from some tea and coffee store or wagon. So, if you will sell our brand, why, you will have all these customers. You may not make so much on each pound, but in the long run you will make more money." Thus this demonstrating helped the dealer's general business as well as promoted his sales of this brand of coffee. Once a field was covered, distribution secured, and demand created, the sales could be kept up by advertising without further demonstrating work.

However, house-to-house demonstrating is usually used to stimulate consumer purchases and increase dealer sales long after distribution in the dealers' stores has been secured. There have been many schemes worked out for this purpose. Of these, one of the most interesting was perfected by a bread baker. He had a corps of women go from house to house carrying a suitcase in which were half slices of bread, each slice wrapped in a piece of paraffin paper. The woman would get the housewife to taste this sample, and at the same time would show her through a booklet describing how that bread was made. Then she would seek to get the housewife's order for a loaf of this brand of bread. On her order the housewife would specify her favorite grocer. All the orders on a certain grocer would then be gathered by the salesmen, and the salesmen would deliver, on the second day following, enough extra loaves so that the grocer could deliver one to each housewife who had ordered and collect from her his full retail price. This system, like every other system of sampling and demonstrating, required very thorough follow-up on the part of the advertiser.

Demonstrating can also be done in stores. Saturday afternoon is a favorite time for this work, as women are likely to be in the store then, and are likely to have a little extra time to taste or try the samples and listen to the demonstrator's sales story. Likewise, country fairs and food shows are strategic places in which to carry on sampling or demonstrating work.

Demonstrating or sampling should not be relied upon alone. Advertising should accompany either plan. Otherwise, the sample is unknown—and therefore a suspected intruder. If its name be familiar and respected, as a result of proper introduction through advertising, then the recipient's attitude is: "Oh, yes—this is a sample of So-and-so. I know about this. I'll try it." To make her "know about it" the manufacturer must tell her about it through advertising.

The harder an article is to understand, the more suitable is sampling or demonstrating. In fact, some things are so difficult of explanation that you cannot convey their desirability through word and picture. Even sampling won't do. You have to demonstrate—to show people not only the article, but how it works. But even if a product is so hard of comprehension that it absolutely requires demonstration, still the ideal system is to combine that with educational advertising. And once you get the public to understand your article you need not continue the big expense of demonstrating—advertising can keep it familiar to the public from then on.

All adjuncts to advertising, such as sampling and demonstration work, are usually taken care of by the advertising department. Some even recommend that the advertising department should also be a clearing-house for complaints. That is debatable, but it is a recognized fact that the advertising department should take care of all sorts of sales aids that come under the head of sales promotion. For instance, the creation of inspirational plans to stimulate the salesman is a function of an all-around advertising department. The sales organization of many a big advertiser is stimulated and kept up to the mark by the ideas that the advertising department puts out. Most of the sales contests are originated by the publicity department.

Lectures often come under the jurisdiction of an advertising department. Lectures are purely educational advertising. They are demonstrations on a big scale. Included in this phase of promotion work are lantern-slides, and, in many cases, motion-pictures. Both these phases, in addition to many others, may properly be among the duties of an advertising department.

CHAPTER XXXII

The Dealer's Store as a Medium

. To link up your advertising with the dealer's you will want to use his store as a medium. You may want to install lithographed signs, window displays, and many other kinds of selling aids inside or outside his place of business. This phase of advertising will require as much time of the advertising department as any other part of the work. For one thing, there is so much danger of waste. So much of this sort of advertising matter seldom gets displayed in the dealer's store in the way it should be.

Manufacturers vie with one another to get matter which is so attractive that the dealer will naturally deem it of sufficient value to deserve a place in the front of his store. Some advertisers give away signs which cost $4.00 each, and that only for a window display. They feel that this is worth the money because they will be sure of a place in the window, and exhibition there will more than pay for the cost before the sign has finished its term of duty. The dealer's window plays a big part as a link between the dealer and the manufacturer's national advertising. Window space is so valuable that in Chicago a syndicate has been formed to lease the window space in certain stores in the down-town district. The syndicate which leases these windows from the store-owners has the right to put into them whatever it desires; so, instead of the manufacturer getting space in these windows for nothing, he has to pay a rental to the syndicate for every minute that his display is installed. This tendency to charge for window space is increasing.

In order better to systematize the use of the dealer's windows, an effort has been made by certain big advertisers to create an organization of men to do nothing else but install window displays. One big association of advertising managers worked for over two years on a plan to start some sort of a machine of this kind, so that the big advertiser could hand out 2,000 window displays, and say: "Here, put these displays into 2,000 windows, according to the following list of stores. We will pay you such-and-such an amount for this work."

The value of dealer displays is based on the fact that when the average person goes to a store for a certain article or articles, if she sees the name of your brand of that article she is likely to specify yours. The trouble is that almost every advertiser seeks to help his sales by this method; and the more signs there are in a dealer's store, the less likely is yours to be seen and the cheaper the dealer's store looks. And so the tendency toward putting all sorts of signs all over the dealer's place of business is on the wane. The tendency these days is to put in only the best signs.

The advertising manager has to take care of this display material. He has to work very closely with the selling organization. There is so much waste in the distribution of this kind of advertising that most of it which is indiscriminately mailed out is unprofitable. But, if the salesman personally makes arrangements for the delivery and installation of the signs, there is little loss. Unfortunately, the average salesman has so many grips to carry that it is hard to get him to carry signs too, so his usual way is to carry a special-order blank, and after he has made arrangements for the purchase of the goods, he asks the dealer what advertising aids he wants. Then he puts down a list on this special-order blank, and he has the dealer write his signature as a promise that he will use this matter conscientiously. Most dealers are honest, and as a result this written promise insures a more efficient distribution and use of the advertising matter.

One manufacturer who tried to distribute a window transfer had 5,000 dealers to whom he sold at least once every three or four months. He ordered only 2,000 of these transfers, in case many of his dealers would not want them. After he had really distributed about 1,000 he had to offer prizes to his salesmen in order to get the remaining 1,000 transfers stuck up on dealers' windows. Yet he had 25 salesmen to help in putting those signs to work. It is easy to buy signs to link up your name with the dealer's store. But the difficulty is to get them utilized by the dealers.

There are four main divisions in the field of dealer displays:

1. Complete window displays.
2. Partial window displays.
3. Outside-of-store displays.
4. Inside-of-store displays.

Full window displays are expensive, and they usually require a separate staff to install them. To make room for a complete window display it is necessary not only to remove what the dealer has in his windows, but frequently to wash his windows. Or it is necessary to arrange definitely with the dealer as to the date on which he will take out his present window display and will have his windows washed. Counting the cost of the display material and the time it takes, a complete window will cost on the average of $4.00 or $5.00. A junior salesman of low salary may well afford to devote his time to this kind of work, but it is more profitable to have a special man to do these jobs than to have a high-salaried salesman spend his time dressing windows.

Among the partial window displays are: cut-outs, which stand up of themselves by means of easels; decalcomania window transfers, which go right on the glass itself and usually stay there a year or so; sign-puts, which are posters on paper, with some sort of a device for sticking them directly on the window-glass; electric signs, usually with a flasher contrivance; mechanical moving signs operated either through clock-work or electricity; and many other similar items. The cost of these different displays varies from 10 cents apiece for a small window transfer, and 75 cents apiece for a large colored cut-out, to $10 apiece for an elaborate mechanical moving sign.

For outside-of-store displays metal signs are probably the most used. These may consist of enamelled signs which, in a fair size, cost about $1.00 apiece, and which are expected to last for five or ten years—or tin signs, which are usually

THE DEALER'S STORE AS A MEDIUM 225

lithographed on thin steel sheets and varnished. The so-called tin signs will cost from 10 cents apiece for a small strip 3 inches deep by 16 inches wide, to 50 cents apiece for the usual-size sign, about 2 feet by 1 foot deep. Of course these prices depend upon raw-material conditions, number of colors, character of design, and quantities. Other outdoor signs on cloth, wood, and paraffine paper are also used.

Effective outdoor signs are secured by supplying the dealer with a bicycle rack or a broom-holder, or some other such useful fixture.

Inside-of-store displays consist of any number of different items, from shelf strips to framed pictures. A shelf strip is a very inexpensive sign, usually made on cardboard about ½ inch deep by 1 foot or so wide, for tacking right on the front face of the shelf board. Cut-outs are also popular for inside-of-store displays, although usually the large-size, expensive cut-out should not be used for interior display, because it does not get enough of an audience to justify its expense and because it is so big that it is in the way of the dealer. Where a window cut-out costs 75 cents apiece for a display standing 3 feet high, a miniature of that can usually be made in one-third size for interior use at a cost of 15 cents or 20 cents, depending upon the color, design, and quantity.

Interior displays also include many devices, such as containers for balls of twine, cases for holding paper-bags, and hats and aprons for the dealers' clerks.

The package itself is a very important item of dealer display as well as of sales value. A package should have eye attraction without violating the principles of taste, because above all a package should be inviting. The right use of color should be the main means of display, plus the proper use of composition. In short, a package should be an almost perfect advertisement, with utmost consideration being given to the fact that it must win favor at a distance. The carton in which packages are placed can be given a word and picture appeal, a color display, and a mechanical design which will make that carton the most effective of all kinds of interior-store displays.

Store displays are very, very expensive, and it is necessary to analyze how much an advertiser can afford to spend per store. This depends on many questions: What are the possible sales per month per store? If the average answer is $4.00, then a display expense per store of $2.00 would not be justifiable. What is the habit of the purchaser of this particular kind of product? Does she come to the store for something of this kind, or does she come to the store knowing exactly what brand she wants? In the former case the expense of proper display would probably be more easily justified than in the latter case.

CHAPTER XXXIII

The Mail as a Medium

Although direct-mail advertising represents a smaller amount of money than publication advertising, it probably engages more thought and time of advertising men. The kinds of direct-mail advertising may be largely divided into two classes: (1) Direct-mail aimed at consumers seeking the actual completion of the sale between advertiser and consumer, and (2) Direct-mail aimed at either wholesaler, retailer, or the salesman, sometimes seeking the actual sales as a direct result, but in the main seeking to influence the channels of selling.

In either event the problems are largely the same. In mail-order selling, direct to the consumer, the catalogue is usually the backbone of the plan. This catalogue may be a general catalogue containing all kinds of merchandise, or it may be special catalogues, each one devoted to a particular class of merchandise.

Direct-mail becomes a powerful adjunct to national advertising when used as a means of opening the dealer's door for the salesman. Here its purpose is largely educational, aimed not so much to make the dealer buy by mail as to make the dealer receptive to the solicitation of the salesman. Frequently in this connection the main use of direct-mail is to sell the dealer on the consumer advertising which is being put behind the product. One of the beneficial results of direct-mail work on the trade is to keep an advertiser's goods before the dealer during the long interval which usually occurs between the salesman's calls.

The basis of any direct-mail work is the mailing list. This must be right. There are many sources from which such a list can be built. Consumer mailing lists can be secured from local dealers, from directories, from society columns of newspapers, from club membership lists, from city and state records, from consumers, and through advertising designed to result in inquiries. Lists of dealers are usually in existence in every line of business, and these lists can be refined by taking the list of actual customers and getting the salesmen to coöperate by furnishing lists of prospects as they find them in their travels.

Given a good mailing list, the problem of direct-mail advertising can be largely divided under two headings: (1) Copy and (2) Method. The copy problem is largely the same as in any other department of advertising, except that more thorough copy is possible, because the recipient of a direct-mail appeal is supposed to read more leisurely than a reader of a publication or other medium. The problem of method is almost as important as that of copy. This problem, in turn, divides itself into questions of How and When. Fortunately, direct-mail advertising permits of tests by which the problem as to copy and method can usually be worked out in an experimental way before the complete expenditure is entailed.

A writer in *System* tells of some interesting tests in direct-mail work, as follows:

"In order satisfactorily to solve the question of postage, a test campaign of several thousand mailing-cards was arranged.

"(1) 1,000 mailing-cards were mailed under 1 cent postage, return card unstamped.

"(2) 1,000 were sent out under one cent postage with the return card stamped.

"(3) 1,000 were enclosed in envelopes and mailed under first-class postage, the return card being stamped as in test two.

"The cards were identically the same, the addressing was done by one person, the 3,000 names were taken from the same list, and the cards were all mailed at one time. Here is the comparative productiveness of the three test campaigns showing interesting results:

"Test 1 pulled 5.2% inquiries at a cost of $.292 per piece.
"Test 2 pulled 17% inquiries at a cost of $.149 per piece.
"Test 3 pulled 34.5% inquiries at a cost of $.102 per piece.

"Next the question of whether the mechanical form of a letter had direct bearing on results arose as an undecided issue. To end the perplexity a unique test campaign was arranged as follows:

"(1) 500 letters signed by the multigraph, without salutation or date.

"(2) 500 letters undated and signed, bearing the form salutation 'Dear Friend.'

"(3) 500 letters with name only filled in, as 'Dear Mrs. Blank,' but they were undated and signed on multigraph.

"The tests were conducted under fair and equal conditions; the same return card was enclosed in each set, and all were mailed to names on the same list, at the same time. The results were:

"Test 1 pulled 12% inquiries.
"Test 2 pulled 12.5% inquiries.
"Test 3 pulled 11.5% inquiries."

Letters which are actually typewritten, either by hand or by an automatic typewriting machine, have been known to pull 68% inquiries, when mailed first-class with first-class stamped return envelope enclosed.

Of the many kinds of direct-mail advertising, the most usual is the letter. Blotters are also good, provided they are well done. Blotters have been very successfully used in the form of miniature newspapers, in the form of calendars, and in the form of tables of helpful information.

Even when a letter is used, a booklet is generally desirable, because a letter should be short, whereas a booklet can contain full information and also can be illustrated. Folders can be used in place of booklets when but few pages are necessary. Broadsides have the advantage of being inexpensive on account of the fact that they can be frequently mailed of themselves, without envelopes. Also they have the advantage of impression, due to their bigness of display when opened out in full size.

Mailing cards are also effective. Frequently a mailing

campaign of four or five pieces, at intervals of ten days apart, may be made most effective by using different kinds of direct-mail matter. For instance: the first mailing may be a letter advising of the sending of a booklet at a later date. The second mailing may be the booklet itself. The third mailing may be a broadside. The fourth mailing may be a mailing card, and the fifth mailing may be a letter with order blank enclosed. Little folders, to be used as "stuffers" for enclosure in regular mailing, almost always pay for themselves, provided that not too much bulk of advertising matter is mailed in each envelope.

There is a tendency toward expensive direct-mail matter in the form of actual books. A volume of 60 or more pages, with board covers, has been found very effective, because it seems so much like a book that the recipient is reluctant to throw it away. Impressive portfolios, sometimes in loose-leaf form with leather or imitation leather-covers, are also forcefully used. When an expensive book of this kind is sent out requiring, as it does, an expenditure of from 50 cents to $2.00 a prospect, it is invariably worth while to pave the way with additional mailing pieces calling attention to the main book.

Where expensive folders are used this same sort of tilling of the soil is frequently an expense that results in ultimate economy through making the main pièce de résistance better received. Actual photographs and imitation photographs are also being used in direct-mail advertising more and more.

House organs are a common kind of direct-mail. Sometimes they take the form of magazines, and indirectly seek to further the interests of a manufacturer or group of manufacturers. Usually they are straight out-and-out house organs seeking to persuade the reader of the policies and desirability of a certain company. Sometimes they are internal house organs seeking to increase and maintain the morale of the workers within an institution. The usual dealer receives so many house organs that only a very few get his attention. A house organ that is not of the highest type of mechanical perfection, as well as editorial appeal, is apt to have very little power. But this same principle holds true in regard to all direct-mail. So much of it comes over the usual man's desk that only the best of it ever sees the light.

CHAPTER XXXIV

A Typical National Campaign

When a manufacturer enjoys practically perfect distribution throughout the country, with his goods on sale in almost every store, the least expensive campaign is the one that is nation-wide and all-inclusive. Here is a typical example of the kind of campaign that is usually worked out in such a case. This instance is based on the actual facts—only the name is fictitious.

In January this manufacturer decided on a policy of national advertising. In September he became a national advertiser. It takes only a moment to make these two statements, but it took years to bring them about, for his goods had been successful without advertising, although they had been sold without brand—without trade-mark—without identity. There is not the slightest doubt but that they would have continued to be successful without advertising. All that advertising was expected to do was to make them even more successful in a shorter space of time.

Advertising has reached its highest development in America because American business men are not content to let the public find out for itself about their merchandise. The task of this advertising, therefore, was to tell to the American public the story of this product as it was known to the trade. If every one of the 400 salesmen tried to tell the story of his goods each day to ten consumers, it would have taken two solid years to tell as many people as were told in one week through 2,000,000 copies of the *Saturday Evening Post*.

At first the advertising counsellors made a trip throughout the country, and called on the major wholesalers in St. Louis, Chicago, New York, and other cities. They went into the

A TYPICAL NATIONAL CAMPAIGN 233

factory buildings and through them and under them and over them. The manufacturer knew the facts, and he revealed them. The counsellors then drew up a preliminary survey of more than 100 pages, and in that survey they set forth all the facts they had found.

Two months later their recommendations were ready, based upon the facts assembled in the report. They presented these recommendations to the executives, and received their whole-hearted approval. A few days later they presented the plans in detail to the directors, and again received an O.K. Two weeks later the complete plan was laid before the district sales executives from all over the country.

How had the advertising counsellors arrived at their recommendations? There was the whole field of advertising to choose from—magazines, newspapers, booklets, circulars, letters, street-car cards, bill-boards, electric signs. Which of these forms of advertising would give the advertiser the greatest value for every dollar spent in advertising? They listed the different forms of advertising in order of their importance. Then they figured how much it would cost to do a thorough job in each medium. Naturally, they found that they must draw the line before they had reached every form of advertising, and so, many excellent forms of advertising—such as street-cars and bill-boards—were not included in this plan. They were not deemed nearly as indispensable as, for instance, magazines and newspapers.

This was the first problem: As this was an organization which sold to dealers in cities, towns, and villages throughout the country, the advertising must "blanket" the country. That meant national magazine advertising. But there are certain centres, the larger cities, where more possible buyers are gathered and where more goods can be sold. Therefore it was necessary to put on extra pressure in those centres. How should that be done? Through the larger city newspaper. That meant a combination of national magazine and big city newspapers.

And the next problem was: How large should the advertisements be, and where should they appear? As to size, investigation had revealed that in this line there were already six manufacturers who used thirteen full pages a year in the *Saturday Evening Post*—one using thirteen pages in color. It was further proved that from the standpoint of mortality, 99 out of every 100 advertisers who used full pages in the *Post* two years previous to that time were so successful that they were large-space users during the previous year, whereas out of each 100 users of smallest space, only 23 continued.

Maximum space certainly seemed best at the start, to assure "brand" distribution by impressing the trade, and to compel attention by startling the public into a knowledge of the trade-name through the "shock" or "drive" method. It was figured that after the trade was persuaded, and the public began to know that this brand was on the market, smaller space might be used.

The plan divided the National Advertising Campaign into two parts—first, advertising to the trade, and second, advertising to the consumer. These were deemed of almost equal importance so far as the success of the campaign was concerned, for each one depended upon the other. It was vital that the trade should know all about this campaign—especially now when the advertising was just commencing. If they had advertised exclusively to the consumer every merchant would, sooner or later, have found it out; but they naturally wanted every dealer to know, at the very start, what a big opportunity this campaign meant for him.

So the opening gun was a letter to the trade announcing the campaign in newspapers, and right on the heels of that announcement came the first newspaper advertisement itself. To keep the interest in this campaign at a red-hot pitch, the first newspaper advertisement, and then the second and third were "smashed" into the leading papers of the country within a few days after the first announcement went to the trade.

There were immediate evidences of quickened interest on

the part of the trade. A merchant in Boston cut the first advertisement out of the *Boston Post*, pasted it on his window and attached a sign directly underneath it. His sign read: "We've got them!" Newspapers called up by long-distance telephone to say that dealers wanted to run their own advertisements on the same page with the next advertisement. Salesmen reported requests for window signs.

The news spread very rapidly. Dealers everywhere were asking the distributers for more information. So within the next few days another phase of the campaign opened up. Directly from headquarters came an announcement letter signed by the president of the company. Then a broadside was mailed to the trade of the country. This showed the large advertisements that were to run in the *Saturday Evening Post*. And yet some merchants were still unconscious of the fact that anything unusual had happened. But when they picked up their favorite trade paper a few days later they found a four-page insert, printed in three colors.

Naturally they began thinking about this manufacturer's salesman. They would have a lot of questions that they would want to ask him. So just to let them know that he was on his way to see them, the salesmen were given special Advance Cards to mail out personally to their respective customers.

As many merchants don't have an opportunity to move about very much, and sometimes they get peculiar ideas, to help the salesman in framing his answers to some of their questions and to provide him with the ammunition that he might want to use in showing how advertising had made his line more desirable than it had ever been before, each representative was presented with a special Sales Advertising Manual, at the time of the Sales Convention at the plant, after the advertising had just begun.

This sales manual included the following features:

1. Description of the purpose of the advertising and the results expected.

2. An explanation of how this advertising did not add to the cost of the goods, but ought to make possible a greater value than theretofore.
3. Showing how the advertising would be of direct benefit in reducing resistance on the part of the retail merchant.
4. Suggestions as to arguments and methods to use in presenting the advertising to the dealer.

As the campaign progressed it was found that the people the salesmen met every day were more and more interested in his house. In order that he could get more news about his organization and about the plant behind him and the merchandise that he was selling, a house organ was started. This contained articles of general interest and a mass of personal news. It told about each other and about headquarters.

To keep the merchants of the country closely acquainted with the progress of the campaign, correspondence stickers were prepared. One was produced for each advertisement that was to be run in the *Saturday Evening Post*, and each in such quantity that one could be stuck on every envelope that went into the mail during a certain period. The sticker called attention to the current advertising. For example, during several weeks before the opening advertisement was to appear in the *Saturday Evening Post*, every letter bore a sticker which read: "Watch for our advertisement in the October 9th issue of the *Saturday Evening Post*." Similar stickers were prepared for all the rest of the *Saturday Evening Post* advertisements and were used in the weeks immediately before their appearance.

Of course, requests for store signs began to pour in. As this had been anticipated an adequate number of these were ready for instant shipment, and for the merchants who wanted to link up their own stores with the national advertising a book of ready-made advertisements was prepared for the dealer's own use in his own paper. Practically all of these

A TYPICAL NATIONAL CAMPAIGN 237

advertisements had a great deal in common with the national advertising.

When he visits a man's store, as he travels in trains, as he sits in hotel lobbies, people ask a salesman about his advertising—is his house a big national advertiser? In anticipation of this every salesman was equipped with a Pocket Album, which slipped into the pocket as easily as a bank-book—no longer, no wider, and about one-sixteenth of an inch thick. It was no burden to carry and it told the story of the national advertising at a glance.

To avoid the danger that impossible results might be expected from the national advertising, the following instructions were given to them:

"We believe that the effectiveness of this advertising is as inevitable as time. But we think it would be a great mistake to build this campaign for any flash-in-the-pan result. Our policy includes the principle that the way to build is to build slowly and right, to stamp our message deeply on the public mind with bigness of impression and sustained continuity.

"We believe, therefore, that we should check the real results at the end of three years, rather than at the end of six months or a year. True, you will get a dealer's stimulus. True, the first six months' results may well justify the effort. But no complete inventory can be taken until the seed takes fruit in the minds of millions of consumers. This work of education will not gain force during the first year, and possibly not during the second year. Therefore we feel that three years must elapse before its effectiveness can be sensibly judged.

"We have, therefore, set these goals as follows, according to the intervals at which the different results may begin to manifest themselves:

    Stimulation of salesmen............... 4 months.
    Stimulation of smaller dealers.......... 7 months.
    Stimulation of factory employees....... 10 months.
    Stimulation of larger dealers............ 12 months.

Stimulation of dealers' clerks..........14 months.
Establishment of consumer acceptance...18 months.
Establishment of public appreciation....24 months.
Beginning of genuine public demand....30 months.

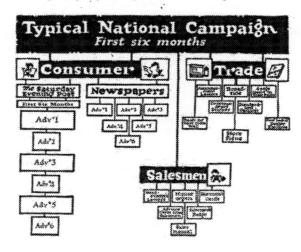

CHAPTER XXXV

A Typical Localized Campaign

In some cases the possible total market of a product may be limited by freight rates, competitive conditions or distribution of manufacturing facilities. In such instances the product's possible consuming population in the United States may be only 25,000,000 out of the nation's entire total. That was the case with a certain food specialty, and, as a result, the advertising campaign had to be localized—national magazines could not be profitably used as 75 % of their circulation would have been wasted.

This is the way the advertising was worked out:

The potential market consisted of 15 cities and their vicinities—15 territorial units, mainly urban. This campaign was opened with a contest among the housewives of one city. The judges were domestic-science experts, including the president of the Housewives League, a Food Specialist of the faculty of Cornell University, and about 15 prominent women.

Two thousand women participated in the contest. It was preceded by conspicuous newspaper advertising before the contest, and afterward, when the product was put on sale at all groceries, more newspaper advertising appeared. Within six months the advertising proved so successful in the first city that the same plan was carried out in another city. The results were similar. The advertising was therefore continued in the first two cities and similar campaigns were started successively in each of the other thirteen territories.

In addition to outdoor and newspaper advertising, many other factors entered into the success of this advertising, such as:

1. A monthly magazine for the salesmen.
2. Numerous pieces of window and store display material, together with thorough directions for their use.

3. Selling talks to the salesmen.
4. Publicity for instilling loyalty and enthusiasm into the factory workers.
5. A new system of house-to-house canvassing.

The handling of the advertising required endless detail, because, as the campaign in each city was started, that particular city required separate, distinct, and special treatment. This compelled the advertising manager to make visits of days, and sometimes weeks, to each of the plants. As a result of these visits, he was able to size up local conditions in a way that permitted him to keep continuous contact with the local manager, and to keep advising him on his local selling conditions with an intelligence based on an intimate knowledge of his own particular local problems.

Among many other sale aids the advertising manager prepared a 20-page book somewhat after the form of the *American Magazine* style of editorial treatment. This was designed to impress the grocer with the desirability of pushing the product. He had every salesman send in the name and home address of every grocer, and he sent a letter to that grocer, over the signature of the salesman who called on him. This letter was followed up by the book, which was also sent to the grocer's *home* address. Fifty thousand of these were mailed. Later a series of merchandising blotters were prepared as a follow-up to the book.

The advertising of course never stopped. Each district manager was furnished every other month with a special schedule, so that he could advise his salesman as to what advertising would be done in his city during the following two months. Here is a typical program for March and April in one of the cities:

"February 23d to March 6th—fourth advertisement appears in newspapers. This advertisement features a little girl with her dolly. It will run in newspapers in the following order: (A schedule followed, showing what newspapers this advertisement would appear in and on what day).

"Attached to this program is a proof of this advertisement. The drawing for this advertisement is the product of one of the best artists in the country. We believe that it will make a real impression on the housewives.

"March 5th to 10th—March issue of the House Organ. This issue is full of interesting articles with a large amount of 'News from the Plants.'

"March 10th—Put out 'Easter' window cut-outs. These cut-outs, which are furnished in both cardboard and paper form, make an opportune piece of window material that every grocer should be glad to feature.

"A sample of this cut-out will be sent you. The cardboard cut-out is very expensive and should be used only in the best stores. The paper copy of same is fixed so it can be easily pasted against the inside surface of the glass in the door or window. We are shipping you the following quantities of these: 450 on heavy cardboard; 900 on paper with stickers.

"March 15th—3-sheet posters are posted all over the city. A real boy and girl give these 3-sheets an appeal which will make them attract real attention.

"March 8th to 20th—fifth advertisement appears in newspapers in the following order: (Schedule followed).

"In this advertisement, the popular 'Baby' is again the subject of the illustration. The head-line is: 'What do his chubby cheeks tell you?' This real youngster is making a real impression on everyone.

"A proof of this advertisement, # BT 5, will be sent you.

"March 22d to April 3d—Advertisement # BT 6 in local newspapers in the following order: (Schedule followed).

"This is another of the advertisements featuring children. Proof of this ad will be sent you.

"April 1st—24-sheet posters are posted according to lists which will be sent you. The subject of this 24-sheet is the same as the 3-sheet posters which appeared in the early part of March.

"April 1st to 5th—April issue of House Organ.

"With every issue this magazine is becoming more and more interesting, and the April number we feel will help every salesman.

"April 5th to 17th—Advertisement # BT 7 appears in local newspapers in the following order: (Schedule followed).

"Proofs of this advertisement which carries on the children series in the same attractive way will be sent you.

"April 10th to 15th—3-sheet posters are posted all over the city. The subject of these posters is a real boy standing at one side, eating.

"April 15th—Put out 'School Girl' cut-outs. Not only are these cut-outs attractive, but they are, perhaps, the most elaborate cut-outs we ever produced.

"Like the 'Easter' cut-out, this 'School Girl' cut-out will be furnished you in two forms—some on heavy cardboard for the best stores—others on paper to paste to the inside of windows in poorer stores. We will ship you the following quantities: 450 mounted on heavy cardboard; 900 on paper with stickers.

"April 19th to May 1st—Advertisement # BT 8 appears in newspapers in the following order: (Schedule followed).

"This is another of the series of ads featuring children. And it is a real piece of copy—so good that it will be remembered long after it has appeared in the papers."

It so happened that this campaign was a rather unusual success in an unusually short time. But this is not typical of the average successful advertising campaign, nor is it to be expected. In fact, in many cases it is not to be desired. Peculiar conditions surrounded this particular product, and this made possible a lightning-like progress.

In the first place, the specialty was an entirely new brand. Progress, therefore, could be measured by the fact that it started off from nothing. In almost every case within six months this brand became the leader in its locality. This was more than satisfactory and seemed to be about as good as could be expected. The natural temptation would have been to let up on the advertising effort and simply keep the brand a little bit ahead of its competitors. But this temptation was resisted.

The advertising was kept up consistently with quite as much force as during the first six months. The sales kept increasing with an occasional slip-back, but on the whole the progress was upward, so that at the end of three years the volume in this brand was three times greater than at the end of six months, and the leadership became more dominant than the leadership that any previous brand had ever enjoyed. This, in turn, brought a new and very vital problem, in that the trade did not like to favor a brand which was so successful that, simply as a result of public favor, it almost monopolized the market. The dealers naturally were sympathetic to the weaker brands, and for that reason were inclined to discourage the progress of the brand that had won first place.

Advertising was by no means the sole cause of this success. The main reason was the superiority of the product. This, in turn, was due to skill in the making and quality of the ingredients. The result was that the brand was really a much better buy for the public because it contained more and better food than competitive brands. But it was the great volume which advertising had helped to build that made it possible to engage the finest manufacturing skill in the country and made it possible to standardize the process to a degree that approached perfection. And it was due to the immense volume that the manufacturer could afford to pay more for his ingredients and yet profitably sell the product at the same price as other manufacturers had to get for their brands.

But a more typical case was the case of another specialty which had been on the market for several decades. Its quality was unusually good, and it had gradually built itself to leadership in certain territories. Its manufacturing process, however, was so superior that it was more expensive to make this brand and, as a result, its price had to be higher than the average competitor's.

The advertising could not cause any rapid strides forward, because already the volume had been built to a considerable height. Then, too, the extra price acted as a constant discouragement to the consumer. The greatest part of the task was, therefore, to keep the present user sold, and to maintain the business that had been built up. In other words, the first function of the advertising had to be defensive—mainly to hold the business and incidentally to add to it. Another rather typical feature entered. There had been a lapse in the advertising for several years. It is a strange fact that when you omit advertising pressure for a year it requires almost twice as much money and twice as much time to bring a brand back to the point where it was before the advertising was discontinued. That is why it is frequently easier to start a new brand than to revive an old brand which has been allowed to sink into semi-oblivion.

One manufacturer found that after only six months' omission of advertising he had to almost double his annual appropriation, and still it took nearly three years to make up the loss in public acceptance and demand.

One of the greatest causes of waste in advertising is the expectation that an advertising success can be made without adequate time, and without the continuous expenditure of enough money to make a definite impression. The old idea was to run an advertisement as a sort of "flier," and then see what the results might be. In 90 cases out of 100 the results were nil and the money was wasted; whereas if a thoroughgoing advertising program of three or five years' duration had been carefully considered, and finally adopted as a definite part of the business policy, the chances would have been almost 99 out of 100 that with a fairly intelligent handling the result would have been a huge success, by which the manufacturer would have lifted himself from mediocrity to leadership.

INDEX

Addington, G. G., quoted concerning color values, 56, 57
Advertising agency, advantages of working through, 174, 175
Advertising campaign, first steps in, 174-176; sample plan, 170-180; example of localized, 239-244; of national, 232-238
Advertising department, functions of, 220
Advertising manager, work of, 174, 175, 223
Agate line, term of measurement, 79
Alexander, H. W., quoted, 172, 173
Analysis, of product, 19-25, 28; of problem, 95-99; of market, 125, 126, 128, 130-132
Appeal, by logic, 22; through "business instinct," 24; by appreciation of consumer's self-interest, 27, 36-39; visual, 86 ff.; price most effective, 103; continuity of essential, 181-186; to women, 200, 241, 242
Automobile advertising, 25, 26, 104, 127, 128, 135, 148

Bargain days, 112, 113
Bauer and Black, examples of advertisements, 171
Bausch and Lamb, examples of advertisements, 53
Bayer's Aspirin, trade-mark and, 15
Beauty appeal, 56, 57
Ben Day screens, 92, 93
Bill-boards, use of, in advertising, 8, 212
Blocking of plates, 70
Blotters, use of, in advertising, 229
Bond Bread, example of trade-name, 14
Boyce Moto Meter, example of advertisement, 213
Broadsides, use of, 229
Bulletins, use of, 190

Cabot Stains, examples of advertisements, 159
Calendering of paper, 75
Car-card advertising, standard size of, 57; uses of, 187, 188, 190, 191; competition in, 209, 210; cost of, 210; examples of, 211; preparing copy for, 214, 215

Cartons, as means of advertising, 225
Caslon type, 77
Catalogues, use of, 141, 143, 220
Central thought, importance of, 180-186
"Charms," examples of advertisements, 211
Cheltenham type, 78
Circular letters, cost of, 22; effectiveness of, 109; early steps in campaign, 157
Circulars, preparation of, 81
Color, value of, 47, 48; chart, 56; choice of, 56-57; printing of, 65, 66
Competition, source of advertising, 2
Competitor, influence of in choice of advertisement, 138, 139
Concreteness, value of, 43, 44, 182
Consignment, selling goods on, 151, 152
Consistency, necessary feature of advertising, 242-244
Consumer, analysis of, 20, 132-137; benefit of advertising to, 3-7, 243; use of statistics in analyzing, 125, 126, 129-131; self-interest of, 34, 36, 182-185
Contests, use of in local campaign, 239
Continuity, essential to success, 18, 211; how to achieve, 181-186; example of "Charms" advertisement, 211
Contrast, value of, 47
Copy, meaning of term, 30; choice of words, 30, 31; danger of "cleverisms," 32; personal element in, 33-35; sincerity in, 37, 38, 101, 106; size and color, 55-57; composition of, 82-85; price emphasis in, 103
Copyright, distinguished from registration, 18
Costs, of advertising, covered by profit, 1-4, 22; problem to new producer, 191, 192
Coupons, use of, 217, 218
Crayon illustrations, 91, 92
Cuts, use of in advertising copy, 68, 81, 82

Dealer, advertising appealing to, 152, 155-158; co-operating with manufacturer, 160, 161, 222-224; influenced by consumer advertising, 156-161, 188; rela-

245

tion to salesman, 169, 170; use of trade journals, 176
Demand, creation of, 24, 25; analysis of, 163
Demonstration, use of, 157, 218–220
Department-store advertising, cost of, 99; price appeal of, 103; example of, 111; window display in, 115; problems of, 117–124; sales, 123, 124; newspaper best medium, 195
Display, appealing to eye, 47–49; to mind, 47–49; combined appeal, 52–54
Distribution, direct to consumer, 138–144, 145, 146; direct through agent, 146–149; local advertising means of, 164–168; successful campaign dependent on system of, 162–164
Dummy, uses of, 81, 82

Eastman Company, advertising of, 12, 13, 83
Edison, examples of advertising, 119
Electric signs, 8, 214
Electrotypes, use of, 72
Em, term of type measurement, 78, 79
Enamelling, of paper, 75
Exaggeration, danger of, 101, 106
Exclusive agencies, use of, 146–152
Eye-display, through contrast, 47; space, 48; color, 48; size, 48; devices of, 87, 88

Fairbanks Company, 12, 45, 59
Fairy Soap, examples of advertisements, 5
Federal Trade-Mark Law, 18
Filene's, examples of advertisements, 111
Font, typographical term, 78
Furniture, selling of, 149

"Gold Dust Twins," 12, 45, 59
Good-will, 154
Gothic type, use of, 77, 78
Gravure printing, 66, 67
Grocery-store advertising, 99

Half-known products, advertising of, 24–29
Half-tones, process of making, 68, 70; kinds of, 70, 71
Hart, Schaffner, and Marx, examples of advertisements, 89
House organs, value of, 230, 231, 236

Illustrations, suggestion by means of, 42; best instrument of attraction, 48; choice of, 86–93; size and cost, 94; *see* Layout
Ingersoll watch, examples of advertisements, 97

Insurance advertising, 104, 128
Intaglio printing process, 66, 67; artistic value of, 67

Jobbers, selling through, 138, 150; advertising essential to success of, 151, 152, 154, 155

Kodak; a trade-name, 11, 12; examples of advertising, 83

Labels, use of, 16; printing of, 65, 66
Letters, as advertising medium, 229
Libby's, examples of advertisements of, 165
Liberty Loan, advertising in, 7
Line-cuts, 86
Line-drawings, 71
Linotype, 80
Lithographic printing, 64–66
Local advertising, newspaper best medium, 195; typical campaign, 239–244
Locomobile, examples of advertisements of, 127
Lowney's Cocoa, examples of advertisements of, 183
"Lux," appeal of advertisements, 11, 12, 57, 90, 186
Luxuries, advertising of, 21–23, 100, 104; display of in department stores, 115

Macey Co., examples of advertisements, 105
Machine finish, in regard to paper, 75
Magazine advertising, benefit to public, 6, 204, 205; choice of cuts for, 71; layout of, 81, 82; illustrations for, 92, 93; best-selling medium, 190; classes of magazines, 205, 206, 208; size of, 206; favored positions, 206, 207
Mail, advertising by means of, 227–231
Mail-order business, 96, 139–148; example of advertisement, 141
Manufacturer, benefits of advertising to, 2–4; creation of dealer demand by, 150, 152–156; distribution problem of, 158–164
Margin, selling to dealers on, 153, 154
Market, analysis of, 201
Measurement of type, 75, 78–81
Media, influences in choice of, 190–192; table of, 193; bill-boards, 212; booklets, 216, 217; bulletins, 213; circular letters, 109; daily newspapers, 194–199; demonstration, 218–220; electric signs, 214; magazines, 204–208; mail, 227–231; movies, 210–212; posters, 213; pro-

grams, 212; samples, 216-218; Sunday papers, 200, 201; theatres, 212
Mennen's, examples of advertisements, 69
Mind-Display, subtlety of, 49, 50; essential qualities of, 51-53; example of, 54
Monotype, 80
Motion, effective in advertising copy, 48, 49
Moving-pictures, made possible by advertising, 4, 6; as medium, 210-212
Multigraphing, 23

Name-Publicity advertising, 8-11; trademark and, 12, 13; when to use, 26, 27; disadvantages of, 36, 37; establishment of, 217, 218
National advertising, 12, 118; salesmanship in, 162-168; steps in campaign, 174-180; typical campaign, 232-238
Necessities, advertising of, 23, 27, 28
Negative method, danger of, 49-53
New products, advertising of, 19-23
Newspaper advertising, choice of cuts for, 71-73; layout of, 81, 82; style of cartoons, 86, 91-93; "Want Column," use of, 100, 101; power of, 110, 112, 158, 160; in planning campaign, 180; advantages and disadvantages of, 188, 197-199; rates, 195-197; classes of advertising in, 196; favored position in, 196; Sunday papers, 200, 201; market analysis by, 201-203

Offset process, 66
"Old Dutch Cleanser," effectiveness of advertising, 12, 16, 18
"Old English" type, use of, 153
"Olivilo," examples of advertisements, 153
Overstocking, danger of, 154, 155

Packages, means of advertising, 225
Painted bulletins, 213; preparation of copy for, 214, 215
Papers, choice of, for printing, 73, 75; table of, 74
Persuasive advertising, advantages of, 8-11, 22, 23, 36-38
Photographs, in illustrating copy, 94, 99; in mail advertising, 230
Photogravure printing, 66, 67
Pianola, examples of advertisements, 129
Pica, printing term, 79
Placing of advertisements, 22, 23, 25, 107, 108, 110, 112
Plates for printing, kinds of, 68, 70-72
Ply, paper term, 75

Point, typographical term, 75, 78
Posters, use of colors in, 56; size, 57; appealing illustrations for, 91, 92; preparation of copy for, 212, 214, 215; examples of, 213; cost of, 212
Presses, kinds of, 64, 66
Prices, cut by advertising, 3, 4
Printing of advertisements, 64-67; Intaglio process of, 66, 67; kinds of plates, 68-73; papers for, 74
Producer, benefit of advertising to, 1-7
Product, analysis of, 19-28, 140, 142
Prospect, analysis of, 19-28, 125-131; aid of statistics in, 128, 130
Prudential Insurance Co. of America, examples of advertisements, 187
Psychology, in advertising, 30-33, 38, 39

"Quaker Oats," transfer from "name" to "persuasive" advertising, 10, 11
Questionnaires, examples of, 133, 135-137

Rates, bulletins, 213, 214; car cards, 210; magazines, 206; moving-pictures, 210, 211; newspapers, 195-197; posters, 213, 214
"Reason-why" advertising, 10, 22
Red Cross, advertising of, 7
Retail advertising, 95-101; price emphasis in, 102, 103; in newspapers, 110, 112, 113; by window displays, 114; manufacturing co-operation in, 115, see Department Stores
Riebel, S. A., quoted, 214
Rotary process, 64-66, 73
Rotogravure printing, 66, 67; Sunday papers and, 200, 201
Routing, process of, 72

Salesmen, importance of advertising to, 169-173; window displays supervised by, 223; equipment of, 235-237
Sales organization, co-operating with advertising department, 109, 170, 172, 173
Sales systems of distribution, 138 ff.
Samples, use of, 43, 110, 216-220
Saturday Evening Post, the, power as advertising medium, 232, 234
Screens, use of in half-tones, 70, 71
Sears, Roebuck Co., successful mail-order business of, 143
Sherbow, Benjamin, quoted concerning type, 77
Siddall, John M., quoted concerning magazine advertising, 203
Silhouette half-tones, 71

248   INDEX

Sincerity, value of, 7, 37, 38, 106, 182
Size, use of, in copy, 48, 55; problems in choice of, 58–61
Sizes, of boards, 75; of car cards, 57; of magazines, 55; of newspapers, 58; of posters, 57; of printing papers, 73; of type, 78, 79
Sizing of paper, 73, 75
Slogans, use of, 18, 185; examples of, 186
Space, value of, 48, 188; factors influencing choice of, 58–63; measurement of, 79
Specialties, advertising of, 100, 104, 109
Statistics, aid of in market analysis, 128, 130, 131
Stereotype, 73
Stock, turn-over increased by advertising, 154, 155; in relation to demand, 163, 164
Street-car advertising, see Car Cards
Style, for copy, kinds of, 45–46, 185, 186
Suggestion, basis of advertising, 39 ff.; by means of illustration, 42; by language, 43–46
System, quoted, 228

Theatre, use of curtain and program advertisements, 212
Timeliness, valuable element in advertising, 134, 135, 178, 180, 197; possible in newspaper advertising, 188; difficult in magazine advertising, 207, 208; example "Peace Treaty" poster, 213
Tooling of plates, 70
Trade characters, examples of, 186
Trade-mark, value of, 12, 13; registration of, 14–16, 18; selection of, 15; establishment of through continuity, 18, 181, 182, 184; examples of, 185, 186

Trade-name, examples of, 16, 18
Trade publications, use of, 176, 178, 179, 208
Type, choice of, 76, 82, 84, 85; kinds of, 78, 79; terms of measurement, 78–81; methods of setting, 80, 81; table of, 8; dummies and layouts, 81, 82
Type page, size of, 81

"Uneeda Biscuit," establishment of name, 12, 15, 26, 213
Units of type, 76
Unknown product, creation of want for, 19, 20, 22, 23

Victrola, examples of advertisements of, 17
Vignettes, 71

Wash-drawings, use of, 91, 92; cost, 94
Waterman's Ideal Fountain Pen, peace treaty advertisement of, 213
Web process, 64–66
Whitman's candies, examples of advertisements, 147
Window display, methods of, 114, 115, 202, 224–226; cost of, 224–226
Women, 80 per cent of shopping done by, 35; use of Women's Magazines as media, 265
Woodbury's Facial Soap, examples of advertisements, 35
Woodcock, D. A., quoted in regard to trade-marks, 13
Wood-cuts, 68, 72
Words, choice of, 31 ff., 43, 44

Zinc etchings, 68, 71, 72

CPSIA information can be obtained at www.ICGtesting.com
Printed in the USA
LVOW080339030312

271257LV00001B/156/P